Making
the Grades

Making the Grades

My Misadventures in the Standardized Testing Industry

Todd S. Farley

PoliPointPress

Making the Grades: My Misadventures in the Standardized Testing Industry

13 12 11 10 09   1 2 3 4 5

Portions of this book appeared in a slightly different form in *Education Week*: "Standardized, You Say?" November 17, 2008, and *Rethinking Schools*: "A Test Scorer's Lament," Winter 2008/2009.

Production management: Michael Bass Associates
Book design: Andrea Reider
Cover design: Debra Naylor

Library of Congress Cataloging-in-Publication Data

Farley, Todd.
    Making the grades : my misadventures in the standardized testing industry/ Todd Farley.
        p. cm.
    Includes bibliographical references and index.
    ISBN 978-0-9817091-5-4 (alk. paper)
    1. Examinations—United States—Scoring. 2. Farley, Todd—Career in test scoring. 3. Business and education—United States. I. Title.
    LB3060.77.F37 2009
    371.26'2—dc22   2009018151

Published by:
PoliPointPress, LLC
P.O. Box 3008
Sausalito, CA 94966-3008
(415) 339-4100
www.p3books.com

Distributed by Ingram Publisher Services

Printed in the USA

Contents

v

For
Donna Fiumano,
my book and my love

Preface

WHEN I FINALLY, *finally*, for-real-this-time, I'm-no-longer-kidding, cut all ties to my cushy job in corporate America, it was to the East Village of New York City that I fled. There, in Alphabet City, amid the ghosts of the angry youth who had helped foster the punk rock movement, and surrounded by the memories of the communists, biker gangs, and homeless who used to regularly make their stand against The Man by rumbling with the New York City police in Tompkins Square Park, I hunkered down to forget how I had been earning my money and to figure out my life.

Standardized testing? *Me?* How did it happen?

The standardized testing industry had never particularly interested me, and at no time in my life had I been scared of its consequences or inspired by its possibilities. In grade school, I remember having to take those statewide multiple-choice tests, and I recall thinking only that they had little to do with my life. In high school, on both occasions I took the SATs (the second time at my mother's insistence), I remember most vividly the fact that the test was seriously inconveniencing my weekly game of Saturday-morning Home Run Derby with Shawn and the Druding boys (when Shawn and I showed up at the testing site the first time, we had baseball gloves but no pencils). Years later I ripped open the seal of my

GRE test booklet and thought to myself, "Perhaps I should have studied? Huh . . . ."

Maybe I was being naive, but I always believed that course work, grades, and the professional opinions of the educators who knew me would matter more to colleges or graduate schools than would some random number produced by a mysterious testing company. I couldn't imagine—and I didn't want to be a part of—any institution of higher learning that would ignore my years of classroom work to instead make a decision about me based on a single Saturday's performance. That didn't make any sense to me, so never as a student did I have to fret about standardized testing.

For the last 15 years, during which time nearly every cent I've earned has come from the standardized testing industry, the topic has not interested me any more than it did when I was a student. I've always had other plans for my life—world travel, writing—and testing has been no more than a way to make a living. While I've rather conscientiously attempted to do a decent job in the business, my heart has certainly never been in it: I've just been some guy doing a boring job to pay the bills. Not, perhaps, a philosophy you would hear many teachers espouse, but it was how I got through the days.

The problem is that the testing world is changing. For years, the work I was a part of seemed innocuous. The tests were written, were taken by students, and were then scored by my ilk at a testing company before some state or federal agency used the results to drive curriculum or formulate education policy. It didn't seem to me, however, that I was involved in deciding the future of individual students, teachers, or schools. It just felt like I was involved in some inscrutable statistical dance that didn't specifically mean very much to me or anyone else. While I was vaguely disappointed in myself for not doing what I wanted in life, I certainly never believed by working in the business that I was doing anything wrong or unethical. It was a job I could make my peace with.

Today, however, my peace is harder to come by. Seemingly every day a different news story shocks me with the increasing importance of standardized testing: lawsuits against the College Board, ETS, and Pearson Educational Measurement over misscored SAT tests that led to students not getting into their preferred colleges; lawsuits from parents in the state of California or the city of New York against the state tests that are keeping their children from being graduated or promoted; lawsuits from the National Education Association (NEA) against the implementation of the No Child Left Behind Act and the massive testing system it advocates.

We are fast approaching a point where the graduation of high school seniors or the promotion of any students will result not only from their classroom work or the opinion of the teachers who spend every day with them but will also hinge on their performance on a single *standardized test* (e.g., the California High School Exit Exam). We are nearing a point where teacher pay and teacher hiring/firing will not be linked to an educator's skill or experience as much as it will be tied to his or her students' *standardized test scores* (as is happening in the Houston and Denver school districts). We are facing a world of education where districts and states are awarded federal funds based not on population or need but instead on regional *standardized test scores* (No Child Left Behind).

Perhaps in theory these are good ideas. Perhaps. However, if you knew what I knew about the industry, you would be aghast at the idea of a standardized test as the deciding factor in the future of even one student, teacher, district, or state. I, personally, am utterly dumbstruck by the possibility. The idea that education policy makers want to ignore the assessments of the classroom teachers who spend every day with this country's students to instead hear the opinion of some testing company (often "for-profit" enterprises) in a distant state is, in my opinion, asinine. It is ludicrous.

If you knew what I knew, you'd agree: I have seen testing companies regularly forgo accuracy and ethics in the name of expediency and profit; I have seen psychometricians who barely speak the language making final decisions about our students' understanding of English; I have seen hordes and hordes of mostly unemployed people being hired as temporary workers to give the scores that will ultimately decide the futures of our students, teachers, and schools. I have seen it all through more than a decade and a half in the business, and does anyone really want me and my kind—for-profit types working at for-profit companies—making decisions about their kids' futures? Hell, even I don't want that, and I'm pretty good at the job.

As far as I'm concerned, it's one thing to use standardized testing to take an overall snapshot of America's students at various grade levels, but it's something else entirely when you're talking about making decisions about individual students, teachers, and schools based on the work I do. That is something else indeed, and it ain't a pretty something else.

You don't believe me? You don't think that the development and scoring of large-scale standardized tests is nothing but a theater of the absurd?

Then let me tell you a story.

Acknowledgments

FOR A LIFETIME of love and understanding, I thank my family (parents Carl and Val, brothers Cary and Chris). And for the friendship, support, and advice they offered as I wrote this book, I sincerely thank Nina Metzner, who first convinced me I was a writer; Sarah Saffian; Sam Swope; Dan Brown (of the *Huffington Post*); Alfie Kohn; Jonathan Kozol; Mike Smolinsky; Fernando and Amy Galiana; Caleb Perkins; my friends in testing, but especially Jesse Miller; my assistants, Bonnie and Junior; my ever-enthusiastic agent, Andy Ross; and the wise and wonderful people at PoliPointPress.

PART

1

2

3

Wage Slave

Scoring Monkey

I **BEGAN TO DOUBT** the efficacy of standardized testing in 1994, about four hours into my first day scoring student responses to a state test. At the time I was a 27-year-old slacker/part-time grad student at the University of Iowa, and my friend Greg had referred me to NCS (National Computer Systems, a test-scoring company in Iowa City) as a good place to get decent-paying and easy work. Soon thereafter, after a perfunctory group interview that entailed no more than flashing my college diploma at an HR rep and penning a short essay about "teamwork" (an essay I'm pretty sure no one read), I had myself a career in "education."

On my first day, we new employees, as well as dozens of more experienced scorers, met at the company's rented property on the north side of Iowa City, a warren of tiny rooms filled with computers in the dank downstairs of an abandoned shopping mall. Within 10 minutes of sitting down, the gent sitting next to me—named Hank, a floppy leather hat perched on his head, a pair of leather saddlebags slung across his shoulder—

confessed he had worked at NCS for years and regaled me with stories of his life. In no time he told me how he had overcome his nose-picking habit (a dab of Vaseline in the nostrils) and offered to show me the erotic novella he was writing, beginning to pull it from a saddlebag. I politely declined and wondered what I'd gotten myself into.

Other than Hank, around me was a bunch that looked no better. I had dressed how I thought appropriate for the first day of a new job (a pressed pair of khakis, loafers, a buttoned-down blue shirt), but all around my colleagues were slumped like bored college students and mid-1990s slackers in sweat pants and ripped jeans. A whole lot of heads seemed like they had not lately been shampooed; lots of faces looked groggy and uninterested.

The building itself also failed to inspire. We were below-ground, 12 people sitting in our small room around two islands of six computer monitors each, the only windows about eight feet in the air and offering a view of the tires on the cars out back. Occasionally we could see the shoes of people walking by. The room was lowly lighted by phosphorescent bulbs and smelled antiseptic, like cleaning products and the musty industrial rugs that covered the floors. I couldn't imagine I could continue to work there, a man of my grandiose literary ambitions. My only hope was that the job itself would prove interesting.

After perhaps an hour's worth of idling about, waiting for management to seat everyone and file paperwork and start the computers, we began our task: the scoring of student responses to open-ended questions on standardized tests. The six people at my island of computers would score a fourth-grade reading test from a state on the Gulf of Mexico, the tests of those 9- and 10-year-olds from the Deep South being scored by this group of mostly white, midwestern adults. Before we began, however, we were trained on the process by our supervisor/"table leader," Anita.

Anita first showed us the item the students had been given, a task requiring them to read an article about bicycle safety before directing them to make a poster for other students to highlight some of those bike safety rules. Some of us mentioned it seemed like an interesting task, having the students use their creativity to show their understanding of bicycle safety by drawing a poster instead of asking them multiple-choice questions. I nodded to myself, smiling, approving that this first standardized test question I'd seen in years was open to so many possibilities. The question was definitely not rigid or stringent, and it allowed the students to respond in myriad ways.

Next, Anita explained the rubric we would use to score the student work (a rubric, or "scoring guide," is the instructions given to the professional scorers on how they should mete out credit to the student responses). She pointed out how easy the task would be to score, as it was a dichotomous item where students were given either full credit or no credit. If a student's poster showed a good example of a bicycle safety rule (like riding with a helmet or stopping at a stop sign), full credit was earned. If a student's poster showed a poor example of bicycle safety rules (like riding with no hands or riding two abreast in the road), no credit was earned. Finally, Anita showed us training papers, actual student work that had earned either full or no credit. She showed us 20 or 30 "Anchor Papers," examples of posters that had earned the score of 1 and others given the score of 0. Eventually she gave us unscored papers to practice with, reading the responses on our own and individually deciding what score to give. After we discussed the Practice Papers as a group and Anita was convinced we all understood the scoring rules, it was time to begin.

At that point I was operating under the impression the item was relevant and interesting. I also thought the rubric was absolutely clear and would be a breeze to apply. And from my experience scoring the Practice Papers, I expected to have absolutely no difficulty scoring the actual student responses. At that point, it was all so clean and clear and indisputable I would certainly have been counted among the converts to the idea that standardized testing could be considered "scientifically based research" (to which the No Child Left Behind Act alludes more than 100 times). At that point, I had no doubt I was involved in important work that could produce absolute results.

And then we started to score.

The thing about rubrics, I discovered (and would subsequently continue to discover over the years), is that while they are written by the best intentioned of assessment experts and classroom teachers, they can never—never!—come remotely close to addressing the million different perspectives students bring in addressing a task or the zillion different ways they answer questions. If nothing else, standardized testing has taught me the schoolchildren of America can be one creative bunch.

I bring this up because the very first student response I would ever score in my initial foray into the world of standardized testing was a bicycle safety poster that showed a young cyclist, a helmet tightly attached to his head, flying his bike in a fantastic parabola up and over a canal filled with flaming oil, his two arms waving wildly in the air, a gleeful grin plastered on his mug. A caption below the drawing screamed, "Remember to Wear Your Helmet!"

I stared at my computer screen (the students filled out their tests and those tests were then scanned into NCS's system for distribution to the scorers), looked at my rubric, and thought, "What the #@^&$!?!" In preparing to score the item, we'd all agreed how to apply the rubric and had addressed what seemed like simple issues: credit for good bicycle safety rules, no credit for bad ones. It had seemed so clear.

Looking at my screen, I muttered to myself, held both hands in the air in the universal sign of "Huh?" and flipped through the Anchor and Practice Papers while awaiting a revelation. Certainly the student *had* shown an understanding of at least one bicycle safety rule (the need for a helmet), which meant I was to give him the score of 1. On the other hand, the student had also indicated such a fundamental misunderstanding of a number of other cycling safety rules—keeping a firm grip on the handlebars, not biking through walls of fire—I couldn't see how I could ever award him full credit. I was actually more worried about the student's well-being than I was concerned with his score.

I held my palms up. I mumbled. I flipped through the training papers. Eventually Anita stood behind me, looking at my screen.

"What are you going to do here, Todd?" she asked.

"Good question," I said.

"Does the student show an understanding of a safety rule?" she asked.

"One safety rule," I said.

"And that means you're going to give it what score?" she asked.

"A 1?" I said, looking over my shoulder at her.

She nodded. "Yup."

"*Really?*" I asked her. "We don't care that as a result of following these 'safety rules' the student is almost certainly going to die?"

She laughed. "I think he was having fun, and he certainly knows how important helmets are."

"Yes, he does," I agreed. "Now let's hope he's wearing a nonflammable one when he crashes his no-hands bike into the burning oil."

She smiled, but less enthusiastically. "We don't make the rules, Todd, we just apply them. The state Department of Education says understanding one safety rule earns the student full credit, so we give them full credit."

I shook my head. "We don't care about the context? We count one good safety rule among three bad ones the same as we do one good rule?"

Anita smiled, perhaps ruefully. "One good safety rule earns full credit," she said. She turned to head back to her own computer, and I watched as she walked away. Hank looked at me, shrugged his shoulders, and smiled. One of the other scorers leaned in toward me and grinned.

"Basically," he said, "we are a bunch of scoring monkeys. No thought required."

"Just click," Hank added, making a motion with his mouse finger. "Just click."

They each nodded to me, shaking their heads slowly up and down, bemused looks on their faces. I realized the two of them had definitely drunk the NCS Kool-Aid.

So as Anita insisted, and for reasons that were clear to me but also hard to believe, I clicked on the 1 button, and the response was scored. In the parlance of NCS, I had officially become a "professional scorer," which seemed a slightly exaggerated title for the work I was doing. The poster of the helmeted daredevil slid off my screen and was replaced by another.

Many of the student responses *were* easy to score. Most students simply showed one safety rule (a biker stopped at a stop sign, another using hand signals to indicate their direction), and I would give those responses full credit. Others ignored safety rules entirely (showing a biker doing a wheelie in the middle of the street, for instance, or drawing *unhelmeted* cyclists jumping over fiery moats), and I gave those responses no credit. Other students earned no points for using the blank poster only as an opportunity to sketch, and there were enough doodles of family pets and "best friends forever" to reconsider the brilliant idea of having fourth graders draw pictures as a part of their tests.

Many of the student responses, however, were befuddling, and we scorers might not know what safety rule was being addressed. Sometimes the handwriting was hard to decipher, and for lengths of time the group would unsuccessfully ponder over a word like *grit* before giving up (later someone would yell "right," their mind having subconsciously solved that puzzle even though a score had long ago been given to the response). Other times the drawings were impossible to interpret, and whether we were looking at a biker or surfer or equestrian was not completely clear. On innumerable occasions the scanning of the tests made it incredibly hard to even see the student responses, leaving us leaning forward to squint at vague and fuzzy lines. Some of the drawings did include a caption to emphasize the safety rule ("Use hand signals!" or "Ride single file!"), but others let the drawings stand alone, leaving us confused. We would usually mull over the response on our screens by ourselves before eventually giving up.

"Is this poster indicating bikers should use hand signals?" someone would ask the group. We would huddle around his or her screen.

"I think so," someone would answer.

"No," I might say, "I think they're waving to a friend."

"No," another scorer would disagree, "I think that biker is giving someone the finger!" And we would laugh, but who really knew what that fourth-grade drawing was getting at?

"Really," the scorer sitting there would say, getting frustrated, "is this acceptable or not?"

The rest of us would begin to disperse.

"I . . . ."

"Well, . . ."

"Good luck with that . . . ."

And we would scatter back to our own desks, back to our own screens of problematic, fourth-grade, bike safety hieroglyphics.

Anita would always try to solve the problem. "Is there a clear bike safety rule?" she would ask. "If there is, credit it. If not, don't."

"What if we're not sure?" someone asked. "This *might* be a good rule."

"A clear bike safety rule gets credit," she said. "If not, it doesn't." Anita was a very efficient woman, very direct, and frankly, I liked her less with each passing minute. She acted like it was all *so* obvious, and meanwhile I was attempting to interpret the Crayola musings of a nine-year-old.

Anita's major contribution to our test scoring was in the form of backreading. As we scored the student responses, she would randomly review on her computer screen a small number of the scores each of the six of us were doling out, checking to see we were applying the rules correctly and in a consistent, standardized form. At times this was helpful, as Anita would call us up to her desk to show us a response we may have misscored.

"Remember, Todd," she might advise, pointing to a student response on her computer screen, "we *are* crediting 'riding in single file' as an acceptable safety rule. You gave this response a 0, but it should be a 1."

"Of course," I'd apologize, "Sorry. I'll credit it next time." Her advice was often helpful in remembering the rules and improving my scoring, so in general I was not averse to heeding her counsel. No one necessarily likes to be told they are wrong, but I understood what Anita was telling me was part of my learning curve at the new job. I stoically soldiered on.

Other times I thought Anita was nuts. Near the end of my first day, she called me up to her desk.

"You gave this the score of 0," she said. "How come?"

"I gave it a 0 because it doesn't show any bicycle safety rules," I said.

"That's not a bike at a stop sign?" she asked.

"No, that's a truck at a stop sign," I told her.

"And what's behind the truck?"

"Well," I said, feeling the blood rushing to my cheeks, "behind the truck is a flat-bed trailer, and securely fastened to that trailer by heavy chains is a bike without a rider." The other scorers began to giggle, laughing at my description and realizing Anita and I were on the verge of a small spat. They began to mill around the screen to look at the disputed student response.

"You cannot be telling me that poster shows any understanding of a bike safety rule."

"Yes, I can," Anita said.

"That might be a car-driving rule," I argued, "but it's not a bike safety rule."

"No way, Anita," someone chimed in, "there's not even a rider on the bike."

"Look," she said, her voice starting to rise, "the rule we've been adhering to is that a bike at a stop sign earns full credit."

"It's not a bike," I said. "It's a truck at a stop sign!"

"There's no one on the bike!" someone mumbled.

"Don't worry about it," Anita said. "Remember, all we can do is apply the scoring rules the state gave us. They said a bike at a stop sign is acceptable, so we credit it."

We headed back to our desks, considerable bitching going on along the way. I shook my head but had to laugh.

"My God," I continued, "we're going to wipe out the entire population of elementary students in that state. They're going to be riding into fires thinking they'll be saved by their helmets, going to think they only have to stop their bikes at stop signs if they're strapped to the back of a truck."

"Enough," Anita said. "It's been a good first day, so let's wrap it up. Just score the response on your screen, and then shut your computer down."

I shook my head, smirking. What did it all mean? Could the 1 or 0 that I was punching into the computer really tell anyone anything about these students? It all seemed so random. I decided to score that one final response on my big, first day before I could head home to take out my frustrations on the soccer field. One more response, I told myself, just do one more.

I looked at my screen, and I was amazed.

I'll say this: I do love the students of America. They are often a fascinating and unique bunch. Many of the responses we scored, of course, were pedestrian and predictable, but many others were absolutely captivating. The kid who made the safety poster showing the bicycle strapped on the trailer behind the truck? It's 15 years later, and I still don't know what that little Picasso was thinking. Seriously, was his poster *really* an example of bike riders needing to stop at stop signs? Was it the work of a kid who wanted to draw a picture of his father's pickup but who threw in a bike at the last minute only to remain on task? Was his poster a sly commentary on the fallibility of standardized testing? Who knew?

I thought this as I looked at the screen to score the final student response of my first day at NCS. I could do nothing but laugh at what I saw. The poster, without any caption, showed a stop sign next to an abandoned road, and in front of that stop sign lay the crumpled remains of a bicycle, all twisted tires and busted frame. The poster had nothing else, no other words or bikes or vehicles or people.

What did it mean? Was the student a demented genius, a confused reader, maybe just a bad bike rider? Did the poster mean "You better stop at stop signs or you will crash?" or did it mean "Even stop signs can't put an end to accidents?" Who knew?

Unfortunately, what I did know was what Anita would tell me to score it. I was convinced she would tell me to give it a 1, because she seemed to think any bike at any stop sign should always earn full credit.

I shook my head. I just shook my head and shook my head. No friggin' way, I thought. I am not giving this response full credit for its "understanding" of bicycle safety rules when all it shows is a bike that has been horribly crushed by a horrific accident of some kind.

In front of a stop sign or not.

Uh-uh, I thought. I did the only thing I could do, following the single valuable piece of advice Hank had given me that day: I clicked the X in the top-right corner of the computer screen, shutting it down. That student response would get kicked backed into the system and would, I prayed, get directed to another scorer by the time we began the next day.

I went home, and after playing soccer—after blowing off steam through extended sprints and hearty collisions and many a frustrated howl—I spent the rest of the night railing against NCS and "the system" to a friend of mine, a sweet girl who listened with less interest as the night went on. This girl was a sly one, and eventually she said, "You don't have to work there, you know. You could go back to the university."

I grumbled under my breath, because she knew better. My last job in Iowa City had been at the University of Iowa's business office, where I earned $5.75 an hour to file invoices. While I'd taken secret pleasure in the job because I felt it was reminiscent of Charles Bukowski toiling away at the U.S. Post Office (he and I a couple of great writers struggling against The Man), I quickly left that for NCS because test scoring paid $7.75 an hour. Not only was that two more bucks an hour, it was a nearly 35 percent raise, and there was pretty much no way I was giving that up.

So the next day, for that extra two bucks an hour, I reported back to NCS.

I did it for the money. It would become a familiar refrain.

Numbers

HAVING DISCOVERED my 1994 price—ethics included!—
was just $7.75 an hour, I reported back for my second
day at NCS and began to see what the gig was really all
about. After listening to a cursory, 10-minute review of the
bicycle safety item and scoring rules, we began to read and
score student responses again. I never again saw or heard of
that problematic poster with the busted-up bike "stopped" at
the stop sign that had so annoyed me the day before. It had
been directed to one of my fellow scorers, and one of them—
apparently without much thought, because no one ever mentioned it—scored it, either giving it full credit for so *obviously*
understanding the value of stop signs, or maybe giving it no
credit because he or she believed (as I did) the poster provided
absolutely no clear understanding of anything. While I was curi-
ous what score my unknown coworker might have given the
response, I was even more intrigued to think what some test
developer/education expert imagined that score meant. To me
the poster was absolutely unfathomable, but someone out there
believed it was an indicator of student learning.

Huh, I thought? Well, I guess they know what they're doing.

At that point I may have wondered about the scoring of test items, but never did I waver from the idea there existed virtual legions of education experts—surely in white lab coats, wearing glasses and holding clipboards, probably at some bastion of Ivy League learning—that could make perfect sense of it all. I didn't expect to understand their genius, but I still had faith in its existence. I decided not to worry and continued to score responses.

The more responses we scored, the more comfortable we became. The rules became embedded in our minds, and no longer did we need to review the rubric. Many of the responses remained unsolved mysteries ("What does that word say?" "What is this biker doing?") that we tried and failed to figure out as a group, but plenty of responses were clear. Good bicycle safety rules got credit, and bad ones did not. "Click, click, click" went our computer mice, 1, 0, 1, 0, 1, 1, 0, 0, 0, 1, 1, ad infinitum. Most of the posters were on our screens for no more than seconds. The ones that were confusing we may have looked at longer, but eventually we just clicked a score button, any score button, to make them go away. At that point none of us believed we were making singularly important decisions about students' lives, so whether we gave some confusing bicycle safety poster a 0 or 1 was not the sort of dilemma that slowed us down.

"Click . . . click . . . click" went the computer mice.

Occasionally we would hear advice from Anita ("Remember, a bike on the left side of the sign is credited for stopping; a bike on the right side is not because it has gone past!"), but we heard less and less from her as the days passed. Perhaps this was because we were becoming more capable and confident "professional scorers," or perhaps it was because we had all become so entrenched in our various positions.

Anita knew, for instance, she could give me advice when I'd made a clear oversight with my scoring ("Don't forget to credit two hands on the wheel, Todd!"), but she also knew I was less liberal than she was when interpreting the posters. She knew I probably wasn't going to credit everything she would, so she let those more aberrant responses pass without mention.

If, for instance, I saw a poster with a biker *near* a stop sign ("Full credit!" I could hear Anita screaming) but *with the student's feet still on the pedals*, there was no way I credited that as "stopping." I would score that a 0 without a second thought—regardless of Anita's assertion that the state committee wanted me to give it credit—because I did not believe it showed any student understanding. I'd have no qualms about giving such a poster a 0, because I really believed mine was the truest interpretation of the rubric. Anita may have disputed that, but I never gave her the chance, clicking away without her advice or consent. I was paid to make scoring decisions, so I made them.

Chances were incredibly good in those cases I would never see or hear about the response again. I would click the score I wanted, and unless Anita happened to see it in her random backreading review, the response was gone forever. The score would be recorded.

The only other way such a response *might* be seen again is if it was fed to another scorer to be "second-scored." Second-scoring is the process whereby a certain number of student responses (sometimes 10 percent for an item, sometimes 25 percent, at times even 100 percent of the student samples) are scored by two different readers, so a statistical comparison of "reliability" can be made. Reliability numbers simply show the agreement between readers, which can be shown to the customer/state as proof of the standardization of the scoring process. Without acceptable reliability numbers, there is no evidence the scores are being meted out in any consistent, standardized way. But, if we scorers had a group reliability of 80 percent on some item (meaning we agreed with each other on 8 of 10 samples that had been second-scored), it was proof positive we were doling out the points systematically.

In truth, the reliability numbers could have been the real reason we began to hear less from Anita. Because our group reliability on the bicycle safety item was above the required 80 percent (not that difficult since there were only two available scores to give), Anita had no worries. As long as the reliability remained above the required threshold, all of us scorers and all of our scores were considered good, and all we had to do was slog our way through the remaining 60,000 student responses.

In theory, the system was working wonderfully, although I quickly figured out if 20 percent of those posters were second-scored (which they were for that item), that meant 80 percent of them were not. I realized 8 out of every 10 posters I scored would be seen by me and me alone. There was a good chance, as busy as Anita was with six scorers and all her administrative work, I would be the only person who ever saw most of the student responses appearing on my screen. I recognized at that point I could pretty much score the responses any way I wanted, Anita be damned. Using the training I had been given, as well as my own interpretation of what I thought the rubric really meant, I scored and scored. Then I scored some more, click, click, click.

The mood around my island of computers was resigned, sometimes dark.

"If my friends could see me now," someone would say. "I've finally made it!" We would laugh at the ridiculousness of it, a bunch of college graduates—many with advanced degrees—trying to figure out fourth-grade cartoons.

I discovered my colleagues were an interesting bunch. Hank, it turned out, was a graduate of the Iowa Writer's Workshop, an impressive fact diminished only by his position in life at age 50, a temporary employee earning hourly wages at a test-scoring factory, a guy without a car who seemed to live at the mercy of his hectoring wife and juvenile delinquent daughter. Hank worked at NCS for the simple reason it was the most money he could hope to make in Iowa City: reformed nose pickers who peddled porn and ambled about with leather saddlebags slung over their shoulders weren't worth a lot on the local job market.

Around our scoring island was also a newly minted pharmacist (she spent her break time scanning the newspaper ads for what she called a "real job"), a graduate student doing postdoctoral work in biomedical engineering (he planned on spending only four weeks at NCS, long enough to earn the money he needed until his fellowship kicked in), and a guy studying to take the bar exam. In fact, not only was Vincent studying to take the bar exam, but he was studying during our work day: he kept a law text open on his lap all day, every day, and as many times as Anita asked him to shut it to concentrate on his scoring work, Vincent said, "I'm scoring, I'm scoring" (he did continue to click the scoring button day after day, even as he flipped pages in his texts). He possessed a quite imperious countenance, Vincent did, and ultimately his textbook stayed put. After he later passed the bar exam, never again did we see ol' Vinny.

Other than me, the last fellow in our scoring sextet was Terry, who frankly didn't seem quite right. Terry wasn't dumb, as he spent all his breaks reading one massive tome or another, but he still seemed a bit off. His shirts were normally misbuttoned, and he cinched his pants high above his waist. Although in his 20s, his mismatched socks poked out of orthopedic sneakers, and while he didn't wear a pocket protector, it wouldn't have been surprising if he added one to his ensemble. Terry had just started working at NCS, but he was already beginning to doubt the choice. He wondered aloud, to anyone who would listen, if maybe he shouldn't have taken the job at the cereal factory in Cedar Rapids, which paid less but was so much closer to the home he shared with his mother.

To confirm my diagnosis Terry was a little off, he believed test scoring at NCS could become a career, when in truth it was nothing more than an employment stopgap for three or four months of the year. That was common knowledge because many of the scorers had been working at NCS every fall and spring for a number of years, but not one of them ever ended up with a full-time job. The reality of the work was that most everyone was there only as a way to bide their time until a real career came along, whether that meant at the pharmacy, in court, or (I hoped) in the glossy pages of a national magazine.

Even if Terry did possess a four-year college degree (the NCS HR department was conscientious about this one fact, as if a four-year degree were indicative of having survived some terribly taxing intellectual gauntlet), he seemed too fragile for the job. He was certainly an industrious worker, and he probably cared more about the scoring than anyone else. Unfortunately, Terry also believed he was deciding some poor student's fate with each click of his mouse, which made him more than a little gun-shy. Often, in fact, Terry was so worried about screwing up he was unable to click the scoring button all by himself. Again and again Terry would ask Anita for help ("Is this a hand signal?" or "Do we credit 'S-T-O-O-P' as 'Stop'?"), or he would ask someone sitting beside him what they thought: "Would you give this credit, Vincent?"

Without looking up from his computer screen and/or law text, the attorney-to-be would usually mutter, "Your problem, Ter." Then Vincent *would* raise his eyes toward Terry, as he clearly enjoyed the look of terror that would inevitably sweep across his neighbor's face.

Terry would be at his desk each morning long before our 8 A.M. start time and would remain there until precisely 4:30 P.M., getting up only for his allotted 15-minute breaks twice a day and his 30-minute lunch. He took each announcement from Anita as if it were the word of God, often writing notes to himself about her imparted wisdom (scribbling on a notepad, "What did you say, Anita, about filling out our time sheet today?"). When I say about Terry that something wasn't quite right, I mean he was humorless and worried too much, about each tiny scoring comment Anita made but also about all of NCS's Byzantine rules.

The rest of the scorers in the building, however, were basically going mad with monotony, insane with frustration over our overly regimented lives. We would trudge into work as close to 8 A.M. as possible and would start wrapping up our day as soon as we could. Was 4:20 P.M. too soon to shut down our computers, or should we wait until 4:25? Working all the way to 4:30 was inconceivable. We needed to be out the door at *exactly* 4:30 P.M.

On our two 15-minute breaks and during our 30-minute lunch, most of the roughly 100 scorers would rush upstairs and outside to try to suck in some fresh air and catch a glimpse of the sky, perhaps to share a cigarette or talk to a fellow scorer. For a moment, we could discuss things we cared about, whether music, politics, books, or sports. Still, we couldn't leave the work completely behind, and we laughed bitterly about the seeming randomness of the scoring rules, mocked the students ("No, Suzy, we cannot credit 'Don't chew gum' as a bicycle safety rule"), and complained about the table leaders who kept such a close eye on us, watching to the minute the time we took to go to the bathroom or use the phone. Back inside, as the day progressed, the basement would grow warm and stagnant, a lack of air flow and the combined heat of maybe 100 bodies and 100 computers filling the air, a stench coming from the tiny bathrooms in the hallway that were shared by so many.

I don't mean to whine, as I realize the conditions I'm recounting don't exactly evoke images of the Industrial Revolution.

Sitting on my butt all day and barely having to lift one finger isn't the worst way to make a living. But at the same time, the conditions weren't exactly as exalted as NCS's literature had seemed to describe. In interviewing for the job, I'd seen a brochure that NCS produced—used as a tool both to hire scorers and to show customers the sanctity of the work—showing a huge, open, airy room of smiling test scorers, properly diverse (an African American in one row, an Asian in the next, a Hispanic smiling from the back, although that's not exactly the racial breakdown of *Iowa*), each fascinated by his or her job. Those scorers' obvious good cheer and heartfelt participation in the scoring process—nay, their desire to contribute to the American education system and help students!—nearly leapt off the page.

I, meanwhile, remained stuck in a stinky, subterranean cave with a bunch of bitter slackers who were counting the minutes 'til quitting time. Had you suggested we were involved in "scientifically based research," I would have enjoyed a big belly laugh. The only experiment I could imagine was one testing the limits of human dignity: How far could you degrade a college graduate for the princely sum of eight bucks an hour? Could you return him to elementary school, allowing him to use the restroom only with permission? Could you get him to sit and work in a hot, swampy environment rife with stench? Could you take from him all conscious thought? All free will? All but any ability except to do exactly as told, moving naught but the mouse finger?

Apparently so.

My pal Greg, who turned me on to the job, became a fount of work wisdom for me. He'd been at NCS for years (off and on), and he currently worked as a table leader. Greg had spent a year after college in New Orleans and another in Seattle, and he lived in Holland and Belgium before ultimately settling into Iowa City. There he earned his money from NCS and/or unemployment checks while concentrating most of his efforts on the short films and large canvases he was producing in the basement of his girlfriend's home. Like me, Greg was imagining some sort of glorious and lucrative future in the arts, and neither of us was particularly gung-ho about landing any serious, full-time work. Instead, we killed time at NCS, struggling through the long days, spending our work breaks talking about things we actually cared about, like the championship chances of world soccer powers Ajax of Holland and Manchester United.

When I searched Greg out a week into that first scoring job, I found him supervising a group of six scorers who were arguing about what they were looking at on a computer screen.

"It's a dog," one guy said.

"That can't be a dog. That's a guy."

"But it has fur and a collar!" the first replied.

"Some guys are furry," a young woman said.

"That's not a collar. I think it's a hat."

"What, a bowler?"

"Could be a bowler. Maybe a homburg."

"But it's not a dog because it's standing on two legs."

"Plus," a girl replied, "it's shaking a guy's hands."

"Exactly," the first guy replied jubilantly. "Dogs shake! My dog Pepper—"

"Hold on," Greg interrupted. "Take it easy, people. Let's get an objective opinion here." He pointed to me.

I leaned forward and stared at the screen. I wasn't exactly sure, but I thought I figured it out. "I'd say what you've got there is a bear in a fez introducing himself at a convention."

"It's not a bear!" the first guy howled. "It's a dog!"

"That's not a dog, you mo—"

"Time for break, people," Greg yelled. "Back in 15 minutes!"

Greg's scorers dispersed, continuing their debate along the way, as he and I sat down by his computer. He asked me how things were going.

"Well, at least I get to look at Anita all day."

"The pretty blonde girl?"

"Yup. What's her deal?"

"No idea," Greg said. "She just started."

"What?" I had assumed Anita was some testing expert, but Greg told me it was her first project.

"She's a temp?" I asked.

"Of course," he said. "We all are."

"Everyone?"

"The scorers are temporary," he said; "we table leaders are temps; the two women I answer to are temps."

"There are no full-time employees here?" I asked.

"I think the computer guy's full-time," he said.

I pondered that for a moment. "I can't believe anything gets done without real employees around. I can't believe we temps are going to successfully complete this whole project."

"Depends on your definition of 'successfully.'"

"Yeah," I shook my head. "I can't believe we get acceptable reliabilities, either. Half the responses are bizarre, and some of the scorers seem like idiots."

"Reliability," Greg scoffed. "Don't worry about the numbers. I can make statistics dance."

I looked at him with wide eyes. My break was over and I had to return to my computer, but that was something to consider on the way back to my desk.

With each passing day, what I perceived as the variables of test scoring became more pronounced. Even non-dolts like me made some serious errors. Anita would call me up and point to a bike safety poster on her screen. "What do we have here, Todd?"

"Looks like a poster of a bicyclist with both hands firmly gripping the handlebars over a caption that says 'Keep Your Hands on Tight,'" I'd answer.

"And that deserves what score?" she'd ask.

"Clearly a 1," I would say.

"So why'd you give it a 0?"

"I didn't. I wouldn't. I'd definitely give that a 1. You're saying I gave that a 0?"

And then Anita would point out on her screen both my scorer ID number and the score I had already given: a 0.

"Really?" I'd say. "I can't believe that."

And I couldn't believe it. I couldn't believe I'd so clearly erred when scoring a student response. I always thought the computer had somehow screwed up (either mine or hers), and of course I never remembered seeing the response anyway. Hell, we were each scoring nearly 200 of the posters an hour, so it's not like I could recall that *one* particularly. Or *any* one particularly, for that matter—they were all just a blur. Even if I knew the scoring rules, it seemed occasionally I would flub one simply because they were coming on screen so fast.

Mind you, it's not unreasonable to score that many responses in an hour. If a poster appears in front of you of a girl and her cat, it takes all of a millisecond to click the 0 button. If a poster appears on screen of a boy on a bike wearing a helmet while stopped at a stop sign, it takes only a millisecond to click the 1. And even the more confusing responses didn't take that long to score, because after a couple of seconds' worth of study you just made them go away: click. The only problem with scoring that many responses was first your eyes began to hurt, then you'd become bored and addled and maybe dizzy, and eventually you'd want to cut out your own heart to make your disappointment in life go away (*"This* is what I do for a living?").

Along with the obvious errors made by scoring so quickly, other problems came to light over the weeks. Hank, for instance. And Terry. Those fellows didn't exactly seem to be grasping all the rules. Most of the scorers did (I had a hard time imagining the dude writing his PhD thesis on some arcane medical engineering subject wasn't grasping our two-point rubric), but not all of them.

"Hank," Anita would say, "don't forget to credit 'riding in single file' as a bike safety rule."

"Yes," Hank would say. "Of course."

Then he would look at me, lower his voice, and ask, "Since when did we start crediting that?"

"Day 1," I'd tell him.

"Oops," he'd say. Looking first at Anita over his shoulder, he'd turn back to me with his finger over his mouth, "Shhh . . . ." His eyes would dance, and you knew that Hank had once been a fun and funny guy. He just wasn't a very good test scorer, although he'd been at NCS for years and would remain for many more (he stayed until the day he tried to foist his erotic novella on to the wrong woman, a mistake that led to his being dragged away for good by the HR department).

In contrast, Terry knew the rules, but he had so much extraneous information written on his rubric he could never keep them straight. "Terry," Anita would say, "you failed to credit hand signals again on this poster."

"Oh, no," Terry would blurt, "oh, no." He would scurry up to Anita's desk, shuffling papers as he went, trying to find his instructional note about the difficult "hand signals" problem. "I'm sorry, Anita," Terry would say, on his face a look of sheer horror indicating his belief he may have both ruined a child's life *and* cost himself a job. "I know I have it on here somewhere," Terry would shudder, flipping pages left and right.

Vincent enjoyed these moments enough that he would look up from his textbooks. "Did you look on the rubric, Terry?" he might ask. "Hand signals is the first example given! The first!" Vincent would shake his head with mock indignation, and Terry would blanch.

Given the countless examples I'd seen of bad scoring, including my own, I wondered how the reliability of our group remained above 80 percent. I surmised at some point maybe Anita was fudging the numbers, but that seemed improbable (regardless of what Greg had implied) because the reliability was produced by a computer program, not human calculation.

It should be remembered, however, reliability is no more than a number representing the percentage of *agreement* between scorers. If a group decided to score every student response a 0, they would end up with a reliability agreement of 100 percent. That doesn't mean 100 percent of the papers would be scored correctly, only that they were scored 100 percent consistently.

In the case of our bike safety group, our reliability was above 80 percent even though I knew I was making occasional obvious mistakes (as were Vincent and the PhD-to-be and the pharmacist, which we knew from Anita pointing out the errors), and we also knew what Hank and Terry were doing was pretty much a crap shoot. Sometimes they knew the rules and sometimes they didn't. Still, even if Hank completely muffed the "riding in single file" rule for three straight days, or if Terry was wildly inconsistent with the "hand signals" rule (and maybe the stop sign rule? The single file rule? The two hands on the wheel rule?), only 20 percent of their responses were being second-scored in the reliability pool, so with any luck those particular screwups wouldn't mess with our numbers. I mean, you still had to figure that Hank and Terry scored at least *half* of their posters correctly. That possibility, along with the fact there were only two scores (0, 1) on the bike safety item, made it seem like our reliability percentage would be pretty high by default alone, right?

Wrong.

Greg solved the Mystery of the High Reliability for me near the end of the project. After we finished a postwork game of soccer with the Hawkeye Club, he and I retired to the bar at Joe's Place for a pitcher of Leinenkugel and a chat about our job.

"It's simple," he told me. "If I go into the system and see you gave a 0 to some student response and another scorer gave it a 1, I change one of the scores."

I listened.

"The computer counts it as a disagreement only as long as the scores don't match. Once I change one of the scores, the reliability number goes up."

"The reliability numbers aren't legit?" I asked.

"The reliability numbers are what we make them," he said.

"So," I said, "the only number the customer cares about is a number that can be manipulated by temporary employees?"

He clinked his glass against mine. "It means we'll always have work."

I can't say I was surprised, given Terry and Hank (and me). I sipped my beer. I shook my head. "Man," I said, "I don't mean to sound naive, but I thought we were in the business of *education*." I emphasized that last word as if it were holy.

Greg nodded, thinking for a moment. "Maybe," he said. "But I'd say we are in the *business* of education."

The *business* of education, I thought? Never heard of such a thing.

The Wheat from the Chaff

MY INTENTION in moving to Iowa City had been to establish residency so if I were eventually granted admission into the Iowa Writers' Workshop, I'd only have to pay in-state tuition. Additionally, given my spotty academic record as an undergraduate (2.8 GPA—I cared *a lot* about soccer during my first collegiate go round), I figured I would take classes at the university to get good grades, do some writing, and convince a professor or two to write me a recommendation for the Workshop.

It was an excellent plan, and it actually bore fruit. I earned A's in undergrad courses in nonfiction writing, and a couple of my submissions were extremely well received. I wrote a story about returning to small-town Maine, after college in big-time Montreal, to help my parents run their podunk general store, and it led the instructor to comment during a classroom discussion that the tale had "deeply moved" him. Another story about my last college soccer game—an account that implied both a stunning athleticism on my part as well as a surprisingly well-developed sense of modesty—led to a small debate among three sorority sisters about who was most enamored with the story, a turn of events I was sure was going to lead to my finding true love with at least one of them. Additionally, I used the Maine story to gain a special waiver into a graduate writing course even though I wasn't officially in the program, and my plan seemed to be working beautifully: I was getting instruction, grades, and recommendations. Iowa City and the University of Iowa were proving to be just the place for me.

It was in that confident state of mind in the spring of '95 that I reported to NCS's permanent site on the east side of town to begin my job as a scorer of high school *writing*. To put in perspective how appalling conditions had been at the basement site where I first worked, I was happy to find at the permanent building where I would be working a huge, windowless warehouse that used to be a loading dock.

Regardless of any doubts I may have had about the project (it promised to be tedious, and there *were* those bothersome little questions about the actual validity of the work), my need for easy money easily trumped any ethical issues that might have been bouncing around my head. In the three months since the reading project had ended, I hadn't earned a cent. I was taking one writing class at night, but mostly I spent my days reading (lots of Updike, all of Exley, a few attempts at Gibbons's *Decline and Fall of the Roman Empire*), doing crossword puzzles, and searching out Happy Hour specials in Iowa City's downtown bars. Money was beginning to get tight, and if I was going to ply those sorority sisters in my class with cocktails, I needed some NCS cash.

Greg was employed on the writing project as a table leader, and he warned me I would have to "qualify" to be able to work: After the training was completed, I would have to pass one of two qualifying tests by giving the "correct" score—the same score as the state committee—on at least 14 of 20 essays. Doing so was a requirement of the state that had hired NCS to score its tests.

I scoffed at Greg. I couldn't imagine not being able to qualify to score a *writing* test. It's not like I was Hank or something.

Speaking of Hank, after I abysmally failed the qualifying test (both tries!) and was being shown the door at NCS, whom did I see being walked out beside me? None other than Hank. He, along with me, and perhaps half of the 100 other scorers who had attempted to qualify to score the writing project, had failed and were fired. We flunkies and dingbats were immediately escorted out the door. Because so many of us did not qualify, because the angry horde filing outside was so large, you might think the shame was less significant.

Nope.

Standing at my seat, picking through my Anchor Papers and other materials, searching for my keys and my bottle of water, trying to inconspicuously exit without being seen by Greg, I felt a sense of nearly overwhelming humiliation. The job I could live without (I could always get more money, from another employer or my credit cards or even my parents), but getting canned was incomprehensible, an incredible blow to my pride: *I* wasn't good enough for NCS. *I* didn't know enough about writing. About *writing*!

As a result of that day's events, I went on a bitter bender, about eight hours of drinking and bitching, bemoaning the absurdity of the idea of a man of my possible genius being escorted out of the office by a testing company. A testing company! Preposterous! There was no way an industry that purported to understand writing would not allow *me* to continue working there. It was one thing to be troubled by test scoring, as I was, but another thing entirely to realize the idiotic industry was saying I wasn't smart enough to work in it.

Not smart enough?! *Me?* Absolute bloody blasphemy, I thought, as I sucked down pints of Budweiser and pounded shots of Jim Beam, weaving over the course of the eve from Mike's Tap to the Dublin Underground to the Foxhead. The injustice of it all, the insanity! I railed, I blathered, and I pontificated, imagining (as I got drunker and drunker) retribution and letters to the editor and congressional investigations. By the end of the night—when the beer and bourbon had fully inspired me, had really steeled me to fight for what was right— I had opted for the hunger strike as my means of protest. I'd show those stupid bastards.

At 7 A.M. the next morning I forgave and forgot, when I got a surprising phone call from NCS inviting me back to work. I actually had qualified! Well, I'd *sort of* qualified. Although we'd been told we needed to earn a 70 percent to pass (correctly scoring 14 of 20 essays), a decision had been made by NCS that perhaps 60 percent was good enough after all. Having earned a 65 percent on my first test and a 60 percent on the second (headed in the wrong direction, wasn't I?), I had been deemed a "qualified" scorer.

I was *un*-fired.

I overcame my vicious hangover and made it to work on time that day only after suffering through a scalding shower and imbibing massive amounts of Coca-Cola, but when I got there I saw the room was still only three-quarters full, maybe only half the people who hadn't qualified yesterday having been given the OK to return (including good, ol' Hank, back again). As I took my seat, I nodded hello to a smirking Greg, and I saw the higher-ups at NCS looking around the room, counting heads. Still a quarter of the seats remained empty, and you got the feeling they needed to be filled. Among the management folks, resigned laughter was being shared.

I wondered if the acceptable "qualifying" score was about to be lowered again, but ultimately it was not. We former failures who had earned lowly 60 percent qualifying scores were the only group of losers called back. The other empty seats were later filled by a second group of scorers who had been trained separately and then passed their own qualifying tests.

That was NCS's story, at least, and it was sticking to it.

The writing project had begun exactly as the reading one had. First, the two trainers, Maria and her assistant Ricky, stood in front of the room of 100 people and presented to us the question the students had been given. It was a high school item that prompted those students to write an essay about an "obstacle" they had to overcome.

Next, Maria and Ricky showed us the rubric/scoring guide. It was a six-point, holistic rubric, meaning we would read the student essays and assess them from the low score of 1 to the high of 6 based on the essay's "holistic," or overall, quality: we were to consider certain aspects of the essay—focus, development of ideas, organization, style, grammar—and balance those out before giving the essay its score (see rubric on page 34).

Of course, such repetitive language wouldn't have been used ("excellent, excellent, excellent . . ."). Instead, after some brilliant test developer thumbed through a thesaurus, the rubric changed (see rubric on page 35).

When I first saw the rubric, I thought, "No problem." I could read essays and call them "excellent," "adequate," or "weak." I did briefly wonder how the big bunch of us in that huge room were all going to come to the same conclusions about what "excellent" or "adequate" meant, but I figured the trainers would meld us into one, cohesive, single-minded whole. Or, more truthfully, I didn't care if they did or not—I'd score the essays however Maria and Ricky told me to, because I wanted to get paid.

High School Writing Prompt
Six-Point Scoring Rubric

6 An **excellent** response, the essay includes
Excellent focus and development.
Excellent organization.
Excellent language skills and word choice.
Excellent grammar, usage, and mechanics.

5 A **good** response, the essay includes
Good focus and development.
Good organization.
Good language skills and word choice.
Good grammar, usage, and mechanics.

4 An **adequate** response, the essay includes
Adequate focus and development.
Adequate organization.
Adequate language skills and word choice.
Adequate grammar, usage, and mechanics.

3 An **inconsistent** response, the essay includes
Inconsistent focus and development.
Inconsistent organization.
Inconsistent language skills and word choice.
Inconsistent grammar, usage, and mechanics.

2 A **weak** response, the essay includes
Weak focus and development.
Weak organization.
Weak language skills and word choice.
Weak grammar, usage, and mechanics.

1 An **unacceptable** response, the essay includes
Unacceptable focus and development.
Unacceptable organization.
Unacceptable language skills and word choice.
Unacceptable grammar, usage, and mechanics.

High School Writing Prompt
6-Point Scoring Rubric

6   An **excellent** response, the essay includes
Outstanding focus and development.
Tremendous organization.
Exceptional language skills and word choice.
First-rate grammar, usage, and mechanics.

5   A **good** response, the essay includes
Fine focus and development.
Firm organization.
Nice language skills and word choice.
Solid grammar, usage, and mechanics.

4   An **adequate** response, the essay includes
Sufficient focus and development.
Satisfactory organization.
Suitable language skills and word choice.
Passable grammar, usage, and mechanics.

3   An **inconsistent** response, the essay includes
Unpredictable focus and development.
Irregular organization.
Erratic language skills and word choice.
Uneven grammar, usage, and mechanics.

2   A **weak** response, the essay includes
Poor focus and development.
Fragile organization.
Feeble language skills and word choice.
Unfortunate grammar, usage, and mechanics.

1   An **unacceptable** response, the essay includes
Deplorable focus and development.
Improper organization.
Undesirable language skills and word choice.
Disagreeable grammar, usage, and mechanics.

To begin the training, Maria introduced the prompt and rubric, and then we looked at the Anchor Papers. Maria read each of those essays aloud and explained why the response got the score it did. Additionally, a huge, dark numeral between 1 and 6 was written on the bottom of each essay, so as Maria read them, we scorers would know exactly what score point the essay was being given. Maria would then explain what part of each essay helped earn points and what was missing that kept it from earning more.

I was completely on board, nodding my head yes, yes, yes. Maria and I were in perfect agreement. Some of the scorers would dispute scores, would claim, for instance, that although Anchor #2 was given the score of 6 it *clearly* wasn't as accomplished an essay as Anchor #7, which had only earned a 4, yadda yadda. Maria tried to explain why the original scores were correct and gently but firmly reminded us our job as scorers was to be taught the state committee's rules, not to offer unsolicited opinions.

Opinions, we learned, were not the bailiwick of the professional scorer. Obeying was.

After being trained on the Anchor Papers, we were given 10 practice essays to score on our own. At that point, I must admit, I wanted to cry. Without Maria giving the scores to us, and without that big, dark numeral on the bottom of the page, I didn't know what I was supposed to think about each paper. I would read an essay and have an opinion about it, but since all I was trying to do was mimic the state committee/match my peers/not get fired, I ended up at a loss.

Reading and scoring essays may be easy, but scoring them in a manner matching everyone else in the room is a different story altogether. The issue at that point is not whether or not you appreciate or comprehend an essay; the issue is whether or not you can formulate exactly the same opinion about it as do all the people sitting around you.

When you are trying to do that, individuality is not good. Insight is not good. A deep understanding of an essay's implied meaning is not good. Absolute adherence to groupthink is very, very good.

That's exactly what was going through my head as I looked at Practice Paper #1.

Practice Paper #1

The first-born child, position of honor all over the world. While heirs' to faim and fortune, recipients of whatever glorie a family has. Throughout historie that has been the place of the first child born, to get the best opportunity to suceed.

Regardless of those facts, that doesnt always work out. It didn't work out for me. Even though I'm the first-born son.

In many countries, I would have been the big winner. A boy born first usually makes out. He gets the family money, the best job, the best choices of house and wife. In America, no. it doesnt work like that. In America everybody has to earn things themselves. The progenitors don't attomatically pass it along. If you asked me, thats a pile of crap. Im actually sort of kidding because I do think you should have to earn things yourselfe, but I wouldn't have minded getting some free stuff too.

Instead, what I get as first-born here in Amerca is the chance to be the test run in child raising. I'm the guineau pig for my parents, a child-raising' practice run. If my parents fail when raseing me, they'll improve their chance for the rest of their kids. Because I'l suffer at the hands of my parents so maybe my brothers and sisters will have it easier. I'm like a pincushion of learning for the whole family. Not the same as being a coddled toddler, a family prince, right? However, as bizarre as it is mine is an important part of the family environment (regardless of how disfunctional that mite be.)

A good example is when I, do to very little fault of my own got a somewhat bad grade 2 years ago (okay, I got an F, and maybe I deserved it). Still, my parente's freaked out and grounded me for the summer, thereby depriving me of the TV, video games and musical accompaniements today's child needs. Bye the end of the summer my mother saw how much I'd sufferd so she knew that she couldn't use that punishment again. Because my mother tried and failed that one with me now my sisses and bros wont' have to go through the same thing. The suffering I went through as test dummie means my younger family members are off the hook of that punishment. Its not inheriting a castel but that's my new job as the oldest.

Another bad part of my honored position is that I have to be the responsible one. Since my sister and brothers are yunger than me it falls on me to take care of them when my parents are gone. To make matters even worse is that since my brothers and sister ain't too smart (Im telling it like it is, is all) I have to diligently keep a close eye on them. Even if I do it's often a fruitless task. My sister is always marking up the white karpet with her red pen. A little trick that she says is awesom I say is stupid. When she does it I get in trouble because, as the oldest I'm supposed to be responsible for her. What a load of crap! Like I said before.

Its not ALL bad being oldest. Even if I dont get to attomatically marry the best girl in town I do get to stay out later than my siblings and get to do things they cant. So you ask me about an obstacle. Well you try being the oldest one in a family of four kids. Mostly you get the short end of the stick. Especially if you know how good you would have it in the old days.

I read the paper two or three times and ended up stumped. Sure, I had thoughts about the essay. I could score it. I could give it a 5 or 3 or 1, could call it "good" or "inconsistent" or "unacceptable." That wasn't hard at all. The only hard thing was having those opinions be identical to everyone (or anyone) else in the room.

I read the essay one last time. In *my* opinion, Practice Paper #1 was focused on the main idea of an "obstacle" and had a number of details and examples in support. Of course, I thought it had an inconsistent organization, too, basically rambling all over the place without preparing the reader for what was coming next. On the one hand, the essay did include some good vocabulary words, two or three interesting metaphors, and some sense of voice. On the other hand, it also suffered from myriad misspellings, complete cluelessness regarding the use of apostrophes, and an absolutely butchered sense of sentence structure.

Hmmm. . . . So I was supposed to consider all of those things, good *and* bad, was supposed to balance out all the different aspects of that essay and then give the damned thing one "holistic" score? Great. Worse, the rubric didn't seem to address an essay like this one, where each part of the essay (focus, development, style, etc.) was at a different level than the others.

Still, I would try. Let me see, Practice Paper #1 seemed to have maybe a 5 level of focus (it was *all* about the obstacle of being the firstborn), a 3 level of organization (rather wildly bouncing from sentence to sentence, idea to idea), a 4 level of style (some nice voice, good metaphors), and a 2 (or 1) level of grammar, usage, and mechanics.

Hmmm, I thought, . . . Practice Paper #1 . . . .

Was it a 4?

Maybe.

What about a 2?

Could be.

How about a 3?

It seemed like it, but how was I supposed to know?

Maria had a wealth of advice for us. Compare the essay to the Anchor Papers, she said. Compare it to the descriptions on the rubric, she said. Just read it and trust your gut-level instinct. When those pearls of wisdom didn't completely clarify the entire scoring process for everyone, she tried again.

"Read the essay and ask yourself a couple of questions," Maria explained. "First, ask yourself if the response is an 'upper-half' or a 'lower-half' essay. If it's upper-half, you are going to give it a 4, 5, or 6; lower-half a 1, 2, or 3."

She looked at the group of 100 scorers. No one said a word.

"For instance," she said to the group, "Practice Paper #1. Is that an upper-half or lower-half paper?"

No one really said anything. Papers rustled as they were shuffled about; asides were mumbled underneath breaths.

"Upper-half or lower-half?" Maria said loudly, challenging us.

"Upper!" Some guy replied, aggression in his tone.

"Lower," someone responded, as the crowd tittered.

"Upper or lower?" Maria said. "All of you!"

Everyone replied, the room filled with a chorus of commingled "uppers" and "lowers," neither word winning the verbal vote. The tension in the room ebbed away as many of us smiled and laughed at Maria's upper/lower theory getting immediately disproved.

She wasn't deterred though. "All right," she said. "So this paper seems to be right on the line between upper and lower, meaning what?"

"Meaning we don't know what we're doing?"

Maria replied tersely, ignoring the laughter, "Meaning the paper is going to get either a 3 or a 4, right?"

No reply, just giggling and paper shuffling and muttering from the crowd.

"OK," she asked, "who gave this essay a 3?" Around the room arms went into the air, including mine.

"And who gave it a 4?" More arms shot up.

"And did anyone give it any other score?" Random arms popped up.

"A 5," someone hollered.

"A 1," someone else yelled.

Maria's head snapped in that direction. "A what? Who said 1?"

Her question was met with silence, and Maria's eyes narrowed as she tried to find the perpetrator of such an apparently egregious score. Everyone in that part of the room tried to look innocent.

She turned away, addressing the whole crowd. "Practice Paper #1," Maria announced. "The state range-finding committee says this essay earns the score of 4."

Around the room, some scorers cheered while others moaned. I had settled on the score of 3 for that paper, so I was part of the disgruntled group.

How can that be a 4, I wondered? The rubric said the score of 4 meant a paper was "adequate," and there was no way that essay could be called "adequate." It was disorganized, full of sentence fragments and misspellings.

"That paper isn't 'adequate,'" someone argued. "The sentence structure is terrible!"

A bearded and bespectacled, professorial-looking fellow concurred. "The first sentence is a fragment. The second begins with a relative pronoun that doesn't link to a concomitant main clause. I don't know how we can say that is acceptable."

I nodded smugly, "Uh-huh, uh-huh," as if I agreed completely, and even though I didn't know what a "relative pronoun" was, I still gleaned the grammarian agreed with me that 4 was too high a score for that crappy essay.

"What's a relative pronoun?" I heard someone beside me whisper, and when no one answered, I looked haughtily down the table, tut-tutting such ignorance.

"The sentence structure *is* bad," Maria agreed, "but the essay has other attributes. Good focus, some development."

While some in the crowd nodded yes, agreeing with the score of 4, many shook their heads in silent disagreement, pointing among themselves to different parts of the essay to dispute Maria's claim.

"Another thought," she said. "Consider the essay's 'neighbors.' If you are giving a paper a 4, that means it probably has some 3-like qualities and some 5-like qualities, which is different than giving it a 3 and saying it has 4-like and 2-like qualities. When we say Practice Paper #1 is a 4, that still doesn't mean it doesn't have some 3-like characteristics."

We all pondered that for a moment, largely to no avail. A mousy woman asked a question that, although meek in tone, was barbed in its intent. "For my edification, what exactly would a '3-like characteristic' be?"

Maria was unbowed. "A '3-like characteristic' would be some part of the essay that is considered 'inconsistent,' which is how the rubric describes the 3's," she said. "In this paper, that would be the sentence structure, which we've all agreed is inconsistent."

The professor guy responded, "I wouldn't say it was inconsistent. I would say it sucked."

The room echoed with laughter. Maria said nothing, looking stern.

"So if this is a 4," someone yelled, "then what are its 5-like characteristics?"

Maria perked up. "Excellent question," she responded. "Let's look." She scanned the paper in her hand, tracing the words with her finger. "There are some good vocabulary words. *Progenitor*, *diligent*, *fruitless*—those are nice word choices."

"We're counting *fruitless* as a good word choice?"

"Absolutely," Maria replied. "Good word, nice word. Maybe even 5-like."

Someone yelled out. "I see the words *awesome* and *stupid*, which seem pretty 2-like to me. Juvenile clichés."

"Not to mention *crap*, which is 1-like, as far as I'm concerned," a middle-aged woman added.

A white-haired gent, his lips pursed unhappily, said "I'd give that a 0. Kids today—"

Maria interrupted him, "Nothing wrong with those words."

In our chairs, 100 scorers looked around, waiting for a revelation. How did Maria get so wise?

"Yup," she told us, "It's a 4. The range-finding committee says it's a 4, so it's a 4. Makes sense. 'Adequate' focus and development, better word choice, but also troubles with sentence structure and spelling.

"Yup," she repeated. "A 4. How many of you gave it a 4?"

Perhaps half the hands in the room went up.

"Very good," she said, nodding happily, "very good." The fact half the people in the room had given the essay some score other than 4 didn't seem to faze her.

"And on we go," Maria sang. "Practice Paper #2 . . . ."

"Hold on," a middle-aged fellow said. He seemed quite earnest, staring at the essay in front of him. "I gave this paper a 3, and I'm trying to figure it out."

"Sure," Maria said.

"Can you tell me at what point Practice Paper #1 *becomes* a 4?" he asked. "When does it progress from the score of 3 to 4? What puts it over the top? Is it the word choice? The details? If you could show me exactly where . . . ."

Maria smiled. "I wish it were that easy," she said. "But because we're scoring holistically, we look at the overall response and assess its entirety. There's not a single thing about any paper that makes it a certain score point. It's everything."

The man said nothing, nodding. He seemed to be trying to articulate a thought. "OK. Well, hypothetically then. Can you—"

Maria stopped him short. "We don't deal with hypotheticals. We just don't. If I answer that question for you, I'll have to answer them for everyone else. It'll never end."

The man looked up at her. On his face was a pained look. He had tried to ask a serious question he thought would help him do his job, and Maria had simply shut him down.

A look of disgust swept over his face. "You don't 'deal with hypotheticals'?" he said. "What a joke. This whole damn process is hypothetical." He tossed down his papers to random cheers from around the room.

Maria looked at him for a moment and then turned away. "On we go," she said. "Practice Paper #2, everyone. Upper half or lower half?"

A confident chorus of "uppers" filled the room, as Practice Paper #2 was a lengthy and eloquent essay. There was no doubt it would earn a high score.

"Excellent," Maria said. "It sounds like we're all 'uppers' on this one, which is right. Definitely a 4, 5, or 6."

The room nodded in happy agreement, no question about it. Maybe we *were* starting to figure this out.

"OK," Maria continued, "so is this essay 'upper upper,' 'middle upper,' or 'lower upper'?"

"Oh, brother," a voice trailed off.

Although we knew what Maria meant, no one really said anything.

"People," she goaded us. "'Upper upper,' 'middle upper,' or 'lower upper'? What do you think?"

This time we did reply, the bunch of us blurting out a muddled mess of "upper-uppers," "middle-uppers," and "lower-uppers," no single phrase any louder than the rest.

"I'd say it's a middle-upper," a smiling guy offered, "but a lower-middle-upper, so I'm giving it—"

"No way," a woman answered, joining the fun. "How could you call that lower-middle-upper? This essay is *clearly* upper-middle-upper."

"People . . . ," Maria warned.

She'd lost us already. Our brief, shining moment of standardization was gone as quickly as it had come.

For days this went on, not hours, through two sets of Anchor Papers, three sets of Practice Papers, and two sets of "consensus-building" essays (a title I would call optimistic at best). The score Maria announced for virtually any essay would provoke lively discussions and heated debate (with 100 scorers, there was always *someone* that would disagree with the score given to any paper), and never did a consistent scoring system become clear. At times I would think I got it, and then, wham-o, complete confusion would reign: Maria would be explaining why some essay I thought was a 5 was actually a 4, before then turning around and declaring the next essay—which I *did* think was a 4—was a 5. At that point it was back to the drawing board, time to recalibrate my thought process and start anew. Although it was quite easy to be in the right ballpark when scoring (giving a 5 if Maria said a paper was a 6, or a 3 when she said it was a 2), but to pick the exact same score as the mysterious "range-finding committee" and the rest of the people in the room was not that simple a task.

It was when we began to take the qualifying tests that things really got ugly. People began to realize it was not inconceivable to fail at qualifying, leading to the very real possibility of being shown the door and losing out on our eight bucks an hour. Given eight dollars was plum pay for Iowa City, none of us was going gently into that good night.

Maria told us not to worry, told us to relax and do our best on the qualifying tests. She told us to heed the wisdom she had been gracing us with.

"OK," a guy asked her. "So it's test time, and what you're saying is I should read the essays and . . . ?" He held his fist in the air, counting on his fingers. "One, trust my gut instinct. Two, stick with my original score. Three, compare the essay to the Anchor Papers. Four, compare the essay to the descriptors on the rubric. Five, ask myself upper or lower half. Six, uh, ..."

"Six," someone added, "think about the 'neighbors' of each score point."

"Seven," another said, "pray."

"Does that seem about it?" The guy with now two hands in the air asked Maria.

"Seems about right," she said. "Good luck."

Not surprisingly, a large percentage of the room did not score at least 14 of the 20 essays in the first qualifying set correctly. At that point, with time running out and only one more chance to qualify (by passing the second test), civilized debate came to an end and nerves started to get frayed.

"How can you possibly call Qualifying Paper #1 a 4?" an angry 20-something dude asked Maria. "This essay is definitely better than 'adequate'!"

"The committee called it 'adequate,'" she said, "so it's 'adequate.' That's how it is. Did you compare the essay to any Anchor Papers?"

"I did," the 20-something said defensively. "This paper looks to me exactly like Anchor Paper # 3, which got a 5. I don't see how you can call Anchor #3 a 5 without also calling Qualifying Paper #1 a 5."

"Well," Maria explained, "you should have compared it to Anchor Paper #5, which *did* get a 4. If you'd done that, you'd have scored it correctly."

"And how was I supposed to know which one to compare it to? I compared it to the one that seemed comparable to me."

"Well," Maria said, "you were wrong."

An irritated 30-something woman joined the fight. "I'm with him. It should be a 5," she said. "Look at the vocabulary words in this essay. *Alacrity, perspicacious, audacity.* Those are nice word choices. At least 'good' word choices, if not 'excellent' ones."

"Yes," Maria said, "those are decent word choices. Someone's been doing their SAT prep. But Anchor Paper #5 has nice vocabulary, too. *Nonetheless, succinctly, beforehand.*"

"*Beforehand?*" the woman asked, spitting the word out as if a curse. "*Beforehand* is a good word choice?"

"Pretty good," Maria said.

"You're telling me," the now-angrier 20-something dude said, "that *nonetheless, succinctly,* and *beforehand* are as effective as *alacrity, perspicacious,* and *audacity?*"

"That's what I'm telling you," Maria answered.

The 20-something said nothing, but you could see the gears in his head grinding. "Is there any way," he asked, "I could judge how different vocab words compare to each other? Do you have some sort of reference book I can use to compare pairs or trios of words, so I would know if words are 4-like or 5-like? Whether *apple* and *alleviate* is better than *orange* and *quickly?*"

From the crowd a voice asked, "If *obstruction* and *perseverance* is better than *deed* and *hearty?*"

"Whether," someone said from the back, disgust in his voice, "*quit* and *job* is better than *work* and *earn?*"

"People . . . ," Maria warned.

It just didn't end. As a group, we went over each of the 20 essays in the first qualifying set, sour disputes ensuing over the score given to each one. Always some group of scorers was pissed an essay had been scored what they considered too high or too low, while Maria defended the score with the aid of all those people who had scored it "right." The job was a constant struggle, a bitter battle, with emotional outbursts at every turn.

At some point the bearded, professor dude was apoplectic Maria was saying Qualifying Paper #18 earned the score of 4 based on its adequate "development of ideas." For a full five minutes they argued back and forth about the merits of the essay.

"That's absurd," the professor said, the blood rushing to his cheeks. "To say the essay has 'development of ideas' is absolute folderol."

"I beg your pardon?" Maria asked.

"Folly," he explained pedantically. "Poppycock. Gibberish."

"I know what *folderol* means," Maria said. "I just think you better watch what you say."

At his seat, the professor said nothing, just shaking his head back and forth, completely confident in his own brilliance. With a smug look on his face, he eventually leaned to the man beside him and whispered something, a something that scorer pretended not to hear. The room was completely silent.

Maria broke the tension, asking the professor what score he thought the essay deserved. "I do think it deserves a 4," he replied, to the utter horror of the entire room, "But I wouldn't say it deserves it for its development of ideas. I think . . . ."

To this day I don't know why he thought the essay deserved a 4, because as soon as he said it my heart was filled with hate. Many hearts were.

"Are you telling me," Maria asked, "you gave that essay the correct score and were just arguing about the *reasons* for the score?"

The clever professor suddenly didn't look so smart. He slunk in his seat, blushing, insults being hurled at him from all sides. Most of the people in the room had scored the essay incorrectly and were realizing they had suffered through the ceaseless whining of a guy who had scored it *right*!

"Idiot!" someone yelled.

"Keep your friggin' mouth shut!" another echoed.

A young guy hollered that his actions had been "folderol, absolute folderol," a comic aside that made us laugh and may have been the only thing that kept the professor from being run out on a rail (or at least ostracized in the break room).

Fortunately for the professor, we shifted our rancor to Maria after she soon made an even bigger gaffe. When discussing the final paper in that first qualifying set, she stood in front of us and explained with her usual dispassionate rhetoric that Qualifying Paper #20 was a 4. She told us it had been found to be "adequate," it had "adequate" development and "adequate" language skills. She gave us examples of its "adequateness" and told us the essay was certainly, indisputably, most definitely a 4. That score, of course, thrilled some scorers and disgusted others, engendering the normal debate and dispute, but Maria was absolutely staunch in her belief in the essay's score of 4. She told us it was a 4 and defended it as a 4, never wavering about the correctness of that number and implying with her body language and demeanor exactly how obvious that score really was. *Of course* it was a 4, she was saying.

Then her assistant Ricky sidled up and whispered something into Maria's ear. He handed her a piece of paper, pointing to something on it. Between them, they looked at that paper, then another paper, and then back again to the first. At some point Maria's shoulders slumped. She looked up at the ceiling. She looked down at the ground. For a couple of minutes neither she nor Ricky said a word. Ricky busied himself shuttling papers between piles, making a point not to look at his boss, as Maria stood like a statue.

Eventually she spun on her heel and looked at the crowd. "I'm sorry," Maria began. "I'm very sorry. It was not my intent to confuse you, but I was wrong. The state range-finding committee is calling Qualifying Paper #20 a 3, not a 4."

Whatever she said after that was lost to the uproar of the crowd. Screaming and swearing ensued. Some were yelling with glee that their score of 3 was now correct, while others were despondent their once "right" score of 4 had become, shockingly and suddenly, *wrong*.

Bellowing came from everywhere. "Are you kidding me?" "I knew it was a 3!"

"But I thought you said it was 'adequate'?"

Not a person in that room didn't blurt out something, celebration or condemnation of the new score and disgust over the new development. Even those who had given the essay a 3 were distraught, "right" score or not, because the process itself was proving to be too much. None of it made any sense. The system seemed as standardized as snowflakes, and around the room we were defeated, slumped in chairs, tossing our papers around, bitching loud and long.

It took a while, but the crowd eventually calmed down. There was nothing else to do, nowhere to go. Maria apologized. She said it was an honest mistake and said she wasn't trying to torture us. She said, after begging our forgiveness, that Qualifying Paper #20 was, yes, a 3, and she said we had to deal with it. Then she stood in front of us and explained with her usual dispassionate rhetoric that Qualifying Paper #20 was definitely a 3. She told us it had been found to be "inconsistent," with "inconsistent" development and "inconsistent" language skills. She gave us examples of its "inconsistencies" and told us the essay was certainly, indisputably, most definitely a 3. Maria was absolutely staunch in her belief in the essay's score of 3. She told us it was a 3 and defended it as a 3, never wavering about the correctness of that number and implying with her body language and demeanor just how obvious that score really was.

Of course the essay was a 3, she was saying. What other score could it possibly be?

Off Task

BIG DUMMY that I am, I did fail both qualifying tests on that first writing project, although I was also lucky enough to discover that didn't necessarily preclude me from actually working. As noted, NCS was kind enough to rehire me, *post*–qualifying test failures, as soon as it discovered it was short on personnel. Still, while it may have un-fired me, the company did not do so carelessly. It did so only by putting me on "probation," informing me that although I could come back to work, I could only do so conditionally. When rehiring me, the HR department was very clear a close eye would be kept on me and my kind.

While I wasn't exactly thrilled to return to work bearing the stigma of probation, I did prefer it to unemployment. When I asked Greg, however, exactly what "on probation" meant, he had a good laugh.

"Please," he said. "How many unemployed people with college degrees do you think there are in this town? How many people willing to do this work? Trust me—they're not getting rid of you now."

While I appreciated Greg's optimism, I was glad his opinion was also seconded by my new table leader, Shawn Black. When I asked Shawn what my being on probation meant, she said, "Huh?"

"You're on NCS 'probation'?" she asked. "Never heard of it."

Given that Shawn was my supervisor, the fact she didn't know that she was supposed to keep any particularly close eye on me did help to ease my worries. Unless I was on some sort of "double-secret probation" even Shawn didn't know about, it didn't seem my provisional status was going to be of any great concern.

Good ol' NCS, I thought, you had to give them credit. They truly were consistent and standardized: "Probation" meant exactly as much to them as "qualifying" did.

Having survived the bitter battle for qualification, it was time to score essays for real. The writing project proved fundamentally no different than the reading project, as we spent each day reading student responses and slapping numbers onto them. It was dissimilar, however, in terms of logistics: Instead of six people huddled around an island of computers in a tiny, stinky room, we were 10 people on 10 teams sitting around long, conference tables in a large, musty room. Plus, in lieu of using computers, we would hold in our hands actual student essays, organized and stapled into packets of 20, each packet in a large envelope. Instead of punching an essay's score into the computer, we would read the student response and record its score on a score sheet, filling in the circles of 1 through 6 the way you'd fill in A through D on a multiple-choice test.

My new tablemates were a fine group, quiet and agreeable. Terry sat at one end of the table, having fretted terribly through the entire training process before passing both qualifying tests. Beside him was Scott, a sly guy with a wry smile, his specialty being sarcastic comments. Across the table from me were two former middle school teachers, Maureen and Margie. Sitting to my left was Tammy, an Iowa grad student taking a semester off, a 20-something woman with a big personality and a huge laugh who was nonetheless most notable for her black skin (again, it was *Iowa*). To my right was Kim, a part-time otolaryngology student whose most prominent feature was a remarkable décol-letage. Every day Kim wore a low-cut top, and if I ever hap-pened to glance right, I was invariably greeted by a shot of her tan cleavage. I tried not to stare, but I was in my 20s.

The first day we scored essays, Maria went over the rubric and the Anchor Papers with us again, to "calibrate" the group. She told us each essay would be read and scored by two differ-ent people, so she reminded us to score in a manner that would match our peers. She congratulated us for qualifying and wished us good luck, and then it was time to begin. Each of the 100 scorers in the room was handed a big envelope and told "Go!"

I pulled the packet of essays out of the envelope and began to read the first student response. It was the yawner of a tale of some kid whose parents wouldn't buy him a car for his birth-day, a turn of events our hero imagined was an "obstacle he had to overcome." When I finished reading, I rolled my eyes and wondered what to do. While I was confident in my assessment of the kid as a big baby, I wasn't so sure what score to give his essay. It was certainly developed, explaining in great detail how the poor boy had been slighted, but the essay was poorly organ-ized and grammatically troubled. I looked at the rubric, remembered the training I'd undergone, and considered what everyone else in the room might score the essay. The essay was *probably* a 3 or a 4. It was definitely too good to be a 1 and too bad to be a 6, but I wasn't completely sure it wasn't a 5 (such development!) or a 2 (so many comma splices and sentence fragments!).

Ultimately, I had to choose. Since I thought the essay was "lower half," I decided it was probably a 3, due to its "inconsistency." I wasn't sure, but a 3 seemed right. Picking up my pencil, I filled in the 3 bubble on my score sheet.

About that time, Tammy tapped me on the shoulder and offered me the essay she'd been reading. "Todd," she whispered, "what score would you give this?"

I looked at her and smiled, taking the essay from her hand. "Let me see," I said. I handed her mine. "What would you give *this*?"

So Tammy took my essay and I took hers, and we each read the other's. Tammy's first essay was written by a girl whose Spanish teacher was "mean" to her, and while I found the writer more sympathetic than my boy, I can't say I was completely moved by her plight. Nonetheless, her essay seemed better than my first one, and although not lengthy, it was clear and organized, with few grammatical mistakes.

"What do you think?" Tammy asked.

"Yours seems like a 4."

"A 4?"

"Yup. Seems like an 'adequate' essay. What were you going to give it?"

Tammy shrugged. "I was thinking 3. It doesn't say much."

I shrugged right back. "Maybe you're right."

"Maybe *you're* right."

"What would you give mine?" I asked her.

"I think a 4."

"A 4?" I questioned. "I thought it was a 3."

"Yours has a lot of development and details."

"But the grammar . . . ."

"I liked yours better than mine," she said.

"And I liked yours better than mine."

We gave each other's essays back, Tammy patting my arm. "Real glad we could have this talk, Todd," she said. "It's been a great help." Then she laughed, big and bold, genuine glee at how clueless we both were.

Tammy and I weren't the only ones sharing papers. All around my table, and all around the room, you could see scorers huddled in quiet discussions with their neighbors about what score to give an essay. All of us may have had opinions about each one, but the fear we wouldn't score the way everyone else did made for seriously slow progress. Terry was so fraught with tension he absolutely peppered Scott at his side with questions.

As Terry rambled on, Scott looked at me, held up his hands, and said, "Does he know I have to score my own essays?"

That first day went slowly, oh-so-slowly, as we read essays and worried about the scores, asking our neighbors for their opinions and doubting our own. It made one seriously pine for the clarity of the reading project. While the reading project had troubles of its own, it at least included very clear scoring rules: credit for a good bike safety rule, no credit for a bad one. That's pretty clear stuff.

But you want to talk about a sliding scale? The scale we used to score writing flopped about like a puppy on a frozen pond, going every which way, keeling over and standing up and falling down. In scoring writing, for instance, an essay that had good development of ideas could earn a 6, a 5, a 4, maybe even a 3. An essay that was troubled on the sentence level in terms of grammar, usage, and mechanics could earn a 1, a 2, a 3, perhaps even a 4, 5, or 6. (I don't dispute the idea: Gertrude Stein said of F. Scott Fitzgerald that she'd never met anyone who was such a poor speller, yet he still managed to produce a decent text or two.) The point is that essays with identical levels of ability in certain areas could end up (due to other considerations on the rubric) with significantly different scores. In scoring writing, we were far from having hard and fast rules to live by. It all seemed a little untenable, rather mystifying, and the easiest thing to do was to hand your essay off to your neighbor or plead with your supervisor for help.

The only real assistance I found came in the form of my new supervisor, the delightful redhead, Shawn Black. Shawn didn't bring any more clarity to the scoring process than Maria had, nor was she able to elucidate that indefinable point when one score point turned into the next, but what Shawn *did* bring to the process was diversion: she may have been telling me the same confounding information as Maria ("Scoring is a continuum"; "Don't compare essays to each other—compare them to the Anchor Papers"), but Shawn was so darned pretty when she did so.

As she did her backreading work, Shawn would bring essays back to those of us at her table to discuss our decisions. Kneeling beside me to chat about a score I gave that first day, Shawn questioned me about the student response.

"Todd, what do you think this paper deserves?" she asked. I quickly perused it, a rather lengthy essay about a boy who had difficulties when switching schools. Although I'd read and scored it hours before, I only vaguely remembered the essay. I certainly didn't remember the score I'd given.

"I think it deserves whatever score I originally penciled in," I smiled.

"Well, what do you think it deserves now?" she asked.

"Now I think I'd give this paper a 5," I said, scanning it again. "Yup, a 5."

"Well, you gave it a 4 before," she said.

"I did?"

"Yes."

"And was I right?"

"Then or now?" she asked, a question that even she couldn't help smiling at. "You gave it a 4, but I need you to see it as a 5."

"I do see it as a 5," I said. "At least *right now* I do."

In the project's first week, Maria led daily review sessions each morning, handing out a small packet of essays for us to assess as a group to keep everyone scoring consistently. Unfortunately, those review sessions invariably devolved into the same combative mess that training had been ("The last sentence is a fragment"; "No, it's an artistic choice by a confident writer"; "No, it's a *fragment*"; "No, it's an *artistic choice*"), and they were soon discontinued. Other than the occasional nugget of wisdom Maria would impart ("Score from low to high, not high to low"; "Once a student has earned a score point, they can't lose it"), we heard less from her with each passing day. Instead, we sat at our desks, scoring and scoring, essay after essay, hour after hour, day after day.

The more essays I saw, the easier the job became. Instead of using a six-point rubric, the reality was I was using a three-pointer: 1's were incredibly rare, given only to essays that were unbelievably brief (usually less than a paragraph) or completely incomprehensible, and 2's were unusual themselves, in effect, essays that were really bad but not bad enough to be a 1. Essays that were 6's were also uncommon, and they were very easy to identify, as those essays were usually very lengthy and obviously well written. Essays that earned a 6 were incredibly obvious because they were so good.

In effect, the distinctions I had to make simply came down to deciding between the 3's, 4's, and 5's, which wasn't so hard. To me that ended up being the difference between essays I thought were "not quite OK" (3), "OK" (4), and "better than OK" (5). *That* I could do. I scored and scored.

Even if the job was free from stress, however, it was full of monotony. For the duration of the writing project, four weeks long, I worked eight hours a day for at least five days a week and was expected to score approximately 30 essays an hour. That's right, 30 essays an hour, or *one essay every two minutes*: a two- or three-page essay *every two minutes* about some high school kid's inability to make the baseball team or the cheer-leading squad; a two- or three-page essay *every two minutes* filled with teen angst over unrequited love; a two- or three-page essay *every two minutes* quoting the lyrics of the band Nirvana and bemoaning the death of its lead-singing "god," Kurt Cobain.

It was mind-numbing enough to make me want to weep. Fortunately, I discovered that I didn't actually have to *read* all those essays, or at least not all the way through: Instead, I found I could score reasonably well based on only a quick perusal of each student response, by glancing at the length of an essay, the density of its paragraphs, a random check on its spelling and vocab words. After I'd seen a couple of hundred student responses, I could guess by the end of the first para-graph what score I was going to give any essay, and by the end of the first page or the start of the second, that initial thought had usually been confirmed.

I scanned and skimmed, skimmed and scored. While I may have missed some subtle distinction a student made on the third paragraph of the second page, his or her score still became obvious in the first paragraph of the first page, where I could see how clear the focus was, how fluent the prose, whether the student understood grammar or possessed voice. In no time I could guess at a score, and a quick peek at the rest of the essay would usually corroborate that. Sometimes I changed my mind, but not often.

I wasn't the only one. At break times we would all roll our eyes at the process, at the ambiguity of the scoring itself, but even more at the incredible number of essays we were expected to score every hour, every day, every week. More than one per-son joked, given the reality of what we were doing, that some-one should invent a machine that scored essays based on some combination of length and spelling.

We should have patented the idea: today such automated scoring systems are available for sale. Of course, no one is saying those automated scoring systems do their work based on an essay's length or spelling, and there's all kinds of highfalutin' academic research to prove the validity of those programs. Still, it's important to realize any automated scoring system is taught how to assess essays based on the scores *human readers* first give to student responses. Because those programs cannot actually read, they simply try to mimic what human readers have done. In other words, after I'd scanned/skimmed/scored about 500 essays, an automated system could then be taught to ape what I was doing. It could skim and score an essay based on my earlier skimming and scoring of other essays—sort of a skimming to the second power.

Most impressive about those automated scoring systems, however, is their speed. They are *very* fast. While it used to take me about a minute to scan/skim/score any single essay, the automated programs can assess a student response in as little as seven seconds.

Seven seconds! Wow! Even if those programs *don't* know what an essay says, that's still a helluva time.

I didn't think I was being completely heartless scoring the way I did. I did believe—as quick as my reads might have been—I was scoring accurately. Whatever bubble I penciled in for any essay really was the score I thought it deserved. Regardless, whether I made a perfunctory examination of an essay or a comprehensive study of it, all the student got back was a single digit: 4. The student would never know if my 4 meant he'd written a 5-level essay that was hurt by a weak organization or if he'd written a 3-level essay that was helped by a lively voice. It didn't tell him what was strong about his essay or what was weak. It was just a number.

So if I say I didn't pore over every single word of every single essay I assessed, you have to understand: while some of the essays certainly did affect me—the ones about divorce or illness or loss—mostly they bored me, an endless cacophony of complaints about boyfriend problems, girlfriend problems, mean teachers, homework . . . boyfriend problems, girlfriend problems, mean teachers, homework . . . boyfriend problems, girlfriend problems, mean teachers, homework.

Yawn. I had problems of my own.

For one thing, I wanted to care about *my* writing, not the prose of those bleating teenyboppers. For another, life was passing me by, I could just feel it. Outside the scoring center, spring was blooming, Iowa's fecund earth erupting in flowers and trees, everywhere dive-bombing birds, darting butterflies, and hopping bunnies. The whole world was bright with rebirth, yet I sat trapped inside that dank building, scoring scoring scoring . . . . I swore I could feel my muscles atrophying and my synapses freezing, my life force ebbing away. Meanwhile— desperate to write a great book and desperate to play soccer and desperate to run barefoot through the fields—I sat stunned, stumped, stultifying, hunched at my desk in that big mausoleum of a room, filling in the stinking circles of my stupid score sheet with a friggin' pencil nub, a bitter Bartleby the Scrivener reborn.

At times the work was so dreary it was painful (boyfriend problems, girlfriend problems, mean teachers, homework . . .), and I did whatever I could to get through the days. Nearly every afternoon, facing some huge stretch of hours between lunch and quitting time, I'd be computing my salary. I'd be multiplying the number of hours I'd already worked that week by my paltry hourly wage, figuring a 25 percent loss of the gross to taxes, as I considered whether I could afford to take the next morning off with an imaginary visit to the dentist.

It was even worse when NCS began offering overtime on Saturdays. I could barely stomach 40 hours a week, but the overtime cash was so good I had to consider it. I would get out the calculator again to weigh the plusses and minuses of the extra hours. On one hand, NCS provided free doughnuts for weekend work, and my salary would get bumped up to time and a half: $11.63 an hour! On the other hand, the work absolutely sucked, and many weekend mornings I could be counted on to wake up with a rather significant hangover. The money, however, usually won out (nearly 12 bucks an hour!), and when Saturday work was offered, I could always be found at my desk with pencil in hand, a big bottle of Coke, a few aspirin, and a couple of crullers at my side.

I took relief from the tedium wherever I could find it. Occasionally, when the gods were really smiling on me, I would pull the essays out of an envelope to find the entire packet *blank*, 20 student responses without a single word written on them! (In those cases, whole classes had either missed or skipped the test, but their scores of "blank" still needed to be recorded.) Those packets full of blanks were a salvation for me: If I was expected to score a student response every two minutes, that packet of 20 blanks represented 40 minutes of work. Basically, finding one meant I could sit at my desk and stare off into space for nearly three-quarters of an hour, fantasizing about Shawn Black or the next soccer World Cup, thinking about anything except those darned kids. For me, discovering those packets was like finding Willy Wonka's Golden Ticket.

"Scott," I'd whisper, flashing him the packet of blanks, "sweet relief!"

"Lucky bastard," he'd mutter, showing me his own packet, page after page filled with student words that he actually had to peruse.

The other real reprieve came when I found someone else's completed score sheet in my envelope of essays. Each time a scorer finished a packet, he or she would put the essays and completed score sheet back into the envelope and return it to their table leader. The table leader was supposed to pull out that first score sheet before assigning the packet to a second reader. Occasionally, however, amid all the piles of envelopes in front of them, the table leader would forget to take out the completed first score sheet, and it would end up in the hands of the second scorer. It didn't happen a lot, but it happened enough to give me hope.

The first time I pulled out a score sheet that had been completed by someone else (in the beginning of the project), I felt guilty. I knew very well I wasn't supposed to see what the first scorer had given to those essays, so I took the sheet up to Shawn and immediately turned it in.

"Sorry," I told her, as if I'd done something wrong.

The next time it happened, I was a little less naive and a bit more bored. I may have taken the score sheet back up to Shawn, but I managed to memorize the first five scores penciled in before I did so: 44543. As I walked back to my place at the table, I chanted those numbers in my head like a mantra, 44543, 44543, 44543. Quickly checking the first five essays in the packet, I discovered that 44543 would work. I may not have *completely* agreed with each of those scores, but they were close enough. I penciled in my own 44543.

By the end of the project, finding a completed score sheet had exactly the same effect on me as did discovering a packet of blanks. After a couple of weeks of work, my life had become nothing but essays and ennui, so when I found a completed score sheet I took the easy way out: I copied. I wouldn't even go through the pretense of reading the essays, wouldn't even glance at them. I would simply copy all 20 of the scores from the completed first score sheet on to my second score sheet, trusting the poor fool who'd had to read all those essays had actually assessed them "right." Ultimately, I treated the discovery of completed score sheets as if they were winning lottery tickets.

"Scott!" I'd whisper, waving one to him, rubbing in the fact he'd not recently made such a find.

"Sonuvabitch," he'd grunt. "Why couldn't I be so lucky?"

I knew copying the scores wasn't exactly right. It was clearly a kind of cheating, and it would artificially inflate the reliability numbers. But I also considered the entire process so nebulous that I couldn't imagine my shortcut was hurting anyone, either—it didn't occur to me that whether I slapped a 3 or a 4 down on an essay might actually adversely affect a student. That fact helped to ease my conscience, and so I copied away, copied away, freeing myself up each time for forty more minutes of daydreaming.

For 40 minutes of free time on *that* project, I would have bent a lot of the rules.

Late one Friday afternoon, Maria addressed the crowd, asking for our attention. Her request, however, was met with a palpable apprehension, because we all knew these little speeches never ended well. Worse, it was Friday afternoon, with the weekend *so* close, and we 100 scorers wanted to wrap up our grueling 5-day work week, wanted to put an end to that miserable 40-hour period during which each of us had been expected to read and score some 1,000 essays. A *thousand*, I say.

"Nothing to worry about," she said, sensing our nerves. "In fact, I have an essay to read I think you'll enjoy." It ended up being her greatest gift to us. That essay had us hooked— virtually every person in that room—with its first sentence alone.

" 'Debbie Does Dallas' is a better movie than you might think,'" Maria began, "'less a paean to pornography as an encomium to cinema verité.'"

People chuckled and laughed, sitting up in their chairs, absolutely intrigued, hoping maybe—after thousands of essays—we would finally hear something creative, something original. We did. In fact, not only did we hear something original, but we heard something unique, a comprehensive and comical movie review of the porn classic that had people very nearly falling out of their chairs with delight, three full pages earnestly deconstructing the movie's apt setting, its sublime lighting (most notably in the basement orgy scene), and its innovative musical score. Actually, we were told, not only was the musical score revolutionary, but the "thumping percussion of its humping beat" was probably Oscar-worthy, the movie's lack of even a nomination in that category remaining a black mark on the Academy to that day.

We laughed and laughed as the writer penned a serious movie review, utterly deadpan, subtly discussing sex without ever being crass or vulgar. It was a masterful display on his part—artful, even—and the writer seduced us with both his subject matter and his prose skills. He argued the movie was vastly underappreciated, that it should really be called a "film" and its director an "auteur," positing the only reason it didn't receive more critical acclaim was because "Siskel and Ebert are old farts."

We roared for that young writer, reveling in the pleasure his essay brought us. People were turning red in the face and clutching at their stomachs, laughing so hard they couldn't catch their breaths. Maria read us three full pages, struggling to keep her own composure, the essay remaining steadfastly focused on the film as the writer took us on a fantastic journey from sardonic aside to uproarious punch line. By the time the story had come to its climax, nearly every scorer in the building—including even the white-haired gent who during training had complained about the use of the word *crap* in a response—was pounding on the tables, chanting, "Six! Six! Six!" One or two of the scorers looked a little put off, but overwhelmingly the room was bedlam and joy.

When we had all finally calmed down—and it took a while—Maria smiled and said, "You're welcome." We cheered wildly for her, our beloved Maria, thanking her for that wonderful escape.

Maureen, one of the former teachers sitting across from me, had been one of the few people in the room who didn't seem amused by the movie review. She had blushed at one point, but mostly she sat through it with her mouth set into a stern scowl.

"So, Maria," Maureen asked, "I assume *that* essay gets an 'alert.'"

"Alerts" were rare to the point of nonexistent, the special situation in which a student threatens himself or others with bodily harm. In those cases, the scorer was supposed to "alert" his table leader, and the table leader would forward the response through the NCS channels all the way to the state Department of Education, where the information would be directed to the appropriate principals and administrators so they could intervene. A further caveat is that an essay would only be flagged as an "alert" if the threat was known *only* to us in Iowa City. If the student made a threat but mentioned discussing it with a counselor or parent or friend, we scorers were freed from the responsibility of having to make a dramatic rescue. At that point the kid was someone else's problem.

When Maria first mentioned alerts, some of us had been skeptical. It seemed a little far-fetched we temporary employees hundreds or thousands of miles away from them could make assessments about the health and well-being of those students based solely on 30 minutes' worth of their first-draft writing.

Scott had a good laugh. "My God," he said, "these tests are *such* a powerful tool. First they can assess writing skills and now mental health. Maybe next we'll use them to make career placement decisions or to set up dates for the kids."

Maureen, in contrast, was not so flippant about the crisis. She intended to save the children, every single one, and no sooner had Maria mentioned alerts than did Maureen start flagging essays. Of course, Maureen was a little more fixated on the intervention part of the alert than she was on the threat part, and in no time she had flagged essays and brought them to Shawn to alert her to issues of students swearing, students smoking, and students screwing. Shawn tried to emphasize to Maureen that in the "*rare* case" of an alert, the issue was the student's survival, not his or her behavior.

"I'm sorry," Maureen said, "but I think premarital sex is wrong."

"I understand," Shawn said, "but the point of the alert is to save children who are in imminent danger."

"These children *are* in danger," Maureen said. "Their souls are." She nodded her head up and down, absolutely sure of herself.

By the time Maria read the "Debbie Does Dallas" essay, I'd still never given an alert and didn't know that anyone had. Maureen, however, was still trying, and with the review of "that filthy movie," she thought she'd hit the jackpot.

"No," Maria told her, "that's not an alert. It's not even close."

"Well," Maureen answered, "I'd want to know if my son wrote that."

"That's not the point," Maria told her. "If your son's writing porn, that's your problem, not ours. Seems like a parenting issue to me."

Maureen remained determined. "Can I give it a 0?"

Maria laughed. "Sure thing," she said. "Give all the 0's you want."

Maureen nodded happily. Later she would find that there was no actual 0 bubble on the score sheet, but for the moment she was content.

"So what score should this 'Debbie Does Dallas' essay get?" Maria asked.

"A 0!" Maureen yelled confidently.

"Off task!" came another reply.

"It's brilliant!" Scott yelled. "A 6!" His opinion was met with great approval, a cavalcade of "Six! Six!" echoing from around the room.

Maria ignored the chants and announced her decision. "'Debbie Does Dallas' gets an 'off task.' This response, as great as it is, never talks about an obstacle. Not doing what you're supposed to is considered 'off task.'"

Around the room people nodded, some making notes on their rubric, but at my table Maureen shook her head with disappointment and Scott scoffed, indicating his considerable exasperation.

"I've heard it all now," Scott said to me. "Imagine *we* are calling him off task."

That project was a war of attrition, but eventually we won, each of 100,000 essays getting scored by two different people over the course of four weeks. The scores I couldn't vouch for, but each of the bubbles was at least filled in. All 100 scorers didn't make it until the end of the project, though, and probably 20 of them were lost to vacations and personal issues and better jobs by the time the project was three weeks old. NCS didn't fire anyone, but people just stopped coming in. Kim, the girl sitting on my right, was one of those people, having returned to her family's home in Ames one weekend and just never coming back.

In the project's fourth week, rumors of a new Geico call center opening on the Coralville strip spread through the scoring center, and when the news hit that it paid eight bucks an hour *and* included benefits, it was obvious a mass exodus would ensue. The job might not interest dreamers like me or Greg, but plenty of people needed real employment. I could hear Maureen and Margie, the former teachers across the table from me, having a perfectly predictable conversation.

"Health insurance?" Margie said. "I need it for my kids."

"Me, too," Maureen answered.

By the next day both were gone, happy to have been hired to hawk car insurance instead of score standardized tests. While Margie and Maureen called Shawn to tell her they wouldn't be back, they gave no notice. Not a two-week notice or even a two-hour notice. They needed health insurance immediately, and so they were done with NCS.

As for me, I persevered. Not only did I make it to the end of that project, I started the next one, too. The new project was a small one, with only 20 scorers, but between Shawn and Greg, my friends managed to get me hired. The projects were basically the same, except for one minor difference and one major one: the new project used a four-point rubric instead of a six-pointer (a change that took all of about five minutes to get used to), but (and what a big "but" this was) it turned out to be a "high-stakes" test, too. The scores we gave would determine whether each of a group of ESL (English as a Second Language) students from a midwestern city would graduate from high school. On the 4-point scale, the students needed to get at least a 3 to earn a diploma. Every circle I filled in would determine whether or not a student would pass.

A couple of the essays I scored the first day were from Hmong students (the Hmong is an ethnic group that emigrated to the United States from the mountainous regions of China, Vietnam, Laos, Thailand, and Myanmar), and their stories absolutely crushed me. The essays were terribly written, those students communicating in their second (if not third or fourth) language; the writing was practically incomprehensible, huge run-on sentences that were completely out of control, confusing me entirely about who was doing what to whom, and the spelling was almost always wrong, the meaning barely understandable. Still, as troubled as the essays were, I did manage to glean the gruesome message of each. The first boy told of his father being killed, trapped in a barbed-wire fence and shot dead by military guards as the family tried to illegally flee over a Southeast Asian border, and the second told of a brother lost at sea as an immigrant family tried to float across the Pacific. Each of the stories was devastating, absolutely heart-rending, yet I was supposed to assess the essays based solely on the usual "focus, organization, style, and grammar" crap. Given the rubric I was using, there was absolutely no question that both essays deserved a 1, but *I* didn't think so. Not on my watch.

I can tell you right now that my default score was 3. In two minutes, for not quite eight bucks an hour, I wasn't prepared to say no to some poor kid trying to fulfill his American dream, especially not a kid with a tragic tale. I *couldn't* do it. I *wouldn't* do it. I *didn't* do it. At the same time, though, I wasn't thrilled about meting out wrong scores, either, so at the end of that first day I told Shawn and Greg some imaginary tale about my own family emergency, and I was done with that project as soon as I'd begun: I quit. I didn't stomp off in a huff, but I did slink away feeling dirty. I wasn't going to be NCS's executioner for that hourly wage.

It was then near the end of May, and I was already planning to return to Maine for the summer to work at my parents' general store. When I quit that second writing project, I decided to pack up the car and leave sooner, and heading out of town, I drove past the NCS scoring center for one, final look. Merging on to highway I-80 to begin the long drive east, I thought of my parents, and I thought of my father's career in education. In 1960, when he graduated from the University of Maine, my father returned to his hometown of Rockport and began teaching at the high school. In 1990, my father still talked—then 30 years later—about students he had in that first class, especially the ones he'd not been able to get through to. My father wished he'd tried harder with them, had tried other approaches. While he thought fondly of the many successes he'd had, my father mostly rued his failures, a disappointment that stayed with him for more than three decades.

Thinking of *my* recently completed career in education—the one at NCS, the one where I made fleeting and immediate decisions about children I would never know based on rubrics that were alternately foolish and vague—I didn't exactly see the connection between my job and what my father had once tried to do. I seriously doubted I would ever have the same strong feelings he did when in 30 years I thought of all those bubbles I'd been penciling in.

As I watched the NCS scoring site disappear into my rear-view mirror, I made myself a promise: never again, I vowed, never again.

PART

1

2

3

Management

Table Leader

MY PRINCIPLED "never again" stance to give up standardized test scoring was short-lived. Really, my anti-testing position hadn't resulted from any sense of moral outrage, just the fact I found the whole thing unseemly. I'd always had a pretty healthy ego, and glancing at student responses and lumping them into piles of 1, 2, 3, 4, 5, or 6 wasn't exactly the way I'd planned to make a living. It was a job I felt I could have done starting about the eighth grade, and frankly I felt the whole thing was beneath me.

My parents convinced me otherwise. When I explained to them over the course of the summer how foolish I believed test scoring was, my folks didn't seem particularly put off. Admittedly, my summary of the job didn't include my own tendency toward daydreaming and/or cheating, so my attempt to explain the ambiguity and inconsistency of the work fell on deaf ears. My mother and father heard only that I had a "professional" job at a big corporation, so they were pleased.

When I returned to Iowa City, I ended up right back in the NCS fold. The decision was made easier because my parents didn't disapprove of the work but especially because test scoring was, for me, still the best gig in town. I didn't even have to go through the ruse of pretending to care there—I just needed to click the mouse or fill in the bubbles, which I did off and on for the next couple of years. By the fall of '97, however, my meteoric rise up the ranks of the standardized testing industry was well under way, when after three years of mouse clicking/bubble filling, Maria offered me a supervisory position for an upcoming writing project. The sheen of that plum promotion was only somewhat dulled by the fact virtually every one I knew had already been bumped up to the table leader level. Still, I told Maria I needed to think about it. It's not like I wanted to make a career of testing, and while I was perfectly willing to sit quietly and disinterestedly score student responses, I wasn't sure if I wanted a position of actual responsibility.

Greg convinced me I did. "Dude," he said, "you've got to. It's two more bucks an hour, you're guaranteed an hour of overtime a day, and you won't have to read essays anymore!"

"I won't have to read essays anymore?" I asked. The money was interesting, but that last bit was real news.

"No," Greg said, "you'll be too busy with paperwork."

With that I was sold, and the next Wednesday I was one of 10 people who showed up for the first day of table leader training. We supervisors would spend three days being trained by Maria and Ricky before having to pass a qualifying test, and after that we'd be sitting at the end of a table the next Monday when the big group of scorers showed up for their own training. I was joined as a table leader by my friends Greg, Harlan, and Pete, as well as Caitlin, a new woman whose teaching experience had qualified her to begin her NCS career at the supervisory level.

The training of table leaders proved exactly the same as the training of scorers, in that Maria and Ricky identified the prompt for us, explained the rubric, and went over the Anchor and Practice Papers. The only thing different about that writing assessment was the scoring itself. By the fall of '97, I'd worked on seven or eight different writing assessments, and they'd all been fundamentally the same. Whether four- or six-point rubrics were used, and regardless of the mode of writing (persuasive, narrative, descriptive), after a perfunctory perusal of each student response, we doled out scores based largely on an essay's overall ("holistic") fluency, basically a combination of its development, organization, sentence structure, grammar, usage, and mechanics.

Not quite so for the new project. That writing assessment was a test for eighth graders in a southeastern state, a descriptive prompt ("Describe someone or something who is important in your life") scored on a four-point, "focused holistic" scale. While its rubric did mention the usual development, organization, sentence structure, and grammar, usage, and mechanics, it was especially interested in organization. In fact, the rubric was "focused" on the organization, which was obvious because the organization element was first in every score-point descriptor. The rubric looked like the one on page 76.

At first glance, the rubric looked a bit different from other rubrics we'd used, what with the organization listed first. Still, we figured it would shake out the same in the end, like they all did, but we were wrong. While we managed to get through Anchor Papers #1 through #5 without too vehemently disagreeing with Maria, by the time we got to Anchor Paper #6 (see page 77), we table leaders were scratching our heads. The essay was being given the score of 3, labeled as "good," when it seemed to most of us that it was a pretty lame response.

Writing Assessment
Eighth Grade
Descriptive Mode

4 An **excellent** response includes
Excellent organization, including appropriate use of the
   five-paragraph format.
Excellent focus and development.
Excellent style and sentence fluency.
Excellent grammar, usage, and mechanics.

3 A **good** response includes
Good organization, including appropriate use of the
   five-paragraph format.
Good focus and development.
Good style and sentence fluency.
Good grammar, usage, and mechanics.

2 An **inconsistent** response includes
Inconsistent organization, including the lack of appro-
   priate use of the five-paragraph format.
Inconsistent focus and development.
Inconsistent style and sentence fluency.
Inconsistent grammar, usage, and mechanics.

1 A **poor** response includes
Poor organization, including the lack of appropriate
   use of the five-paragraph format.
Poor focus and development.
Poor style and sentence fluency.
Poor grammar, usage, and mechanics.

Anchor Paper #6
Score: 3

Someone important to me is my cat Ginger. Ginger is my favorite pet, and I have many of them. She is the best one that I have ever had. Without Ginger, I don't know what I would do. I do know that I would be lonely. She is important to me for three reasons, which I'll tell you now. She is fun and loving and soft.

Ginger is fun. Some days after school we play for hours. She likes when I tickle her with a feather. She tryes to bite the feather and I try to see that she can't. If I give her catnip she goes crazy running in circles. I chase her sometimes and we have a blast. I think she's having a blast but I know that I am. Sometimes I take a feather from my pillow and throw it in the air. Ginger watches it like a hawk and then chases it like crazy. I know she likes that. And I like to watch it to.

Ginger is loving too. A lot of the time all we do is sit together. She's a very good sitter. If am bored or lonely, Ginger knows it and helps it. She rubs up against my legs or sits on my lap. Ginger really purrs when I pet her. She likes to be brushed and she likes to be rubbed. I know she loves me by how much she takes care of me and how she loves me when I need it.

Ginger is soft too. Her fur is soft and her skin is soft. Her fat belly is soft too. Where ever I touch ginger my hand feels good. She is like a pillow for me. She is a kind of medicine for me. My heart is cured with Ginger, my soft and furry friend.

Someone or something who is important to me is my cat Ginger. I love her, for at least three reasons. She is fun. She is loving. She is soft. What would I do without her? I don't want to ever know. She is the best cat in the world.

"A 3?" Harlan asked. "Really?"

"Maybe a *low* 3?" Maria said. She didn't seem thrilled with the score, either.

"Are you serious?" Pete asked.

"Remember, it *is* eighth grade," Maria said. "And they do only get 30 minutes to write. These are first drafts."

Caitlin, brand-new to the process, was surprised. "The rubric says a 3 is good," she said. "I taught *seventh* grade, and I wouldn't consider this a very 'good' essay." She made air quotes around the word.

"It's so childish," Greg said. "It's virtually all simple sentences."

"It has no voice," I added, "no style."

"It's *so* formulaic," Harlan said.

Maria looked down at the essay. "I'm not saying I'd give this a 3 in my classroom, either, but that's how we have to score it based on this 'focused holistic' rubric. Most importantly to this state's Department of Education, the essay has a five-paragraph format, with introductory, body, and concluding paragraphs and an introductory sentence in all five of them."

"Yes, a scintillating bit of prose," Greg joked.

But if we disagreed a bit with the score of 3 given to Anchor Paper #6, we were dumbstruck when we saw the score of 2 given to Anchor Paper #7:

Anchor Paper #7
Score: 2

Through the forest I meander, trees on all sides, the smell of fir and pine surrounding me. I trek as quietly as I can, imagining I cut through the forest like the wind, because I know any noise will rouse the birds and the squirrels. They are my friends, these woodland creatures, and I don't want to disturb them. I want them to be as comfortable in their homes as I am comfortable visiting them, and I know I have done well when I hear them squeak and trill. They are not silent from fear because they do not fear me.

I hear the rush of the sea crashing below, Oregon's coastline now no more than a hundred yards away. The salty smell of the ocean accompanies the sound, and I began to anticipate happiness. I am nearly there, my home away from home. My feet tread quietly on a floor of pine needles, and breaks of blue sky are beginning to be seen through the forest's canopy of trees. I am almost there.

When the forest ends, I am at the edge of cliff, a rocky outcropping a hundred feet above the sea. Below me the waves break on the shore, dark water washing up on to lightly colored sand. Driftwood is scattered everywhere. I scan the ocean, and in the distance I see what might be a whale. I see what might be a first whale, and then another, and then I think I see dozens. Although I am not sure, the beauty of this perch is that maybe I do. Whales often breach in these waters.

Following the trail along the cliff, I know how close I am. My troubles begin to fade away. No longer do I worry about my grades or that boy in my class. No longer do I worry about homework or doing my chores. I turn a final corner and there it is, the wooden bench my grandfather carved and placed here. I walk over, dragging my hand across its worn surface, before sitting down and looking out to sea. It is here my grandfather used to tell me that everything would turn out all right, and he was right. He was always right. I sit down to watch the sun set, in this my favorite place.

Harlan was incredulous. "A 2?" he asked. "Out of 4?"

Pete laughed aloud. "I'm supposed to think this isn't as good as Anchor #6?"

Greg scoffed. "This kid needs a publisher, not a score from us."

Maria looked guilty. "I know," she said. "I certainly wouldn't give this a 2, either. The writing may be sentimental, but it's first-draft work from an eighth grader. It's a damned nice response, I agree."

"So?" Harlan said.

"Well, what's the important person or thing in the essay? It's her favorite spot, a fact we don't know until the last sentence. That's not five-paragraph format, is it? There's no introductory paragraph, no introductory sentence—"

"No," Greg said, "it's way more artful than that, building up the suspense nicely and using some beautiful descriptive language."

"Yup," Maria agreed, shrugging. "I know. But this is how they want us to score them."

"*Really?*" I asked. "Rather a tedious five-paragraph essay than a beautifully done three or four paragraphs?"

"It seems that way," Maria answered. She looked at us, resigned. We looked back at her, defeated.

"All we care about is the formatting?" Pete asked.

"That's not the only thing," Maria answered, "but it is the *first* thing."

"Wow," I said, "it almost seems a kid could get a 3 for turning in an outline."

Maria thought about it. "Not quite," she said.

Greg shook his head. "There's gonna be a ton of 2's."

We all agreed, Maria included. We figured we'd see tons of 2's, both the usual below-average essays that earned the score *and* this new category of well-written responses that weren't formatted correctly. It boded ill, we thought. To make matters worse—given that we all thought the rubric itself was screwed up—is that the assessment *mattered*. Although this state test wouldn't decide the individual futures of students the way the previous city assessment I'd briefly worked on had, it was being used to decide what schools and districts in the state were succeeding, which teachers were doing their jobs. Apparently state funding and teacher bonuses would hinge on the results of these tests. When Maria told us that, we were amazed. Nobody stomped out in a huff, mind you, not making 10 bucks an hour, we didn't, but we couldn't believe such decisions would be made based on a test like *that*.

On the second day of training, the state Department of Education representative showed up. When Roseanne asked us how things were going, we all smiled dumbly, exactly as Maria had coached us. "Fine," we said. "Great."

"Good," she smiled. "Do you like our 'focused holistic' rubric?"

"Very interesting," we said, a bunch of Stepford table leaders with plastic grins plastered onto our nodding heads. Regardless of what we may have thought, we knew very well the point of test scorers was to agree, so agree we did. The rubric had been established by the state's teachers after considerable effort, and we *had* to use it. Resistance was futile.

"Very interesting, Roseanne," we told her. "A fascinating change."

Maria did say we thought there would be a lot of 2's if we used that rubric, but that didn't faze Roseanne at all. She was actually pretty smug about it. *Roseanne* didn't think there would be an unusual amount of 2's. *Roseanne* was quite confident in the ability of her state's student writers. Even if there were a lot of 2's, she said, that would be valuable information for the state to have.

Greg couldn't help himself. "Seriously," he said to her, "if we're going to call Anchor #7 a 2, there is going to be a lot of lower-half scores. A *ton* of them."

Roseanne snapped at him, "Why don't you let me worry about that?"

"OK," Greg said, "OK." The rest of us nodded idiotically at her. "Yes, ma'am," we thought, "whatever you say." The customer was always right.

Even if we disagreed with the scoring system, however, we table leaders were not particularly stressed about the project. We weren't even too worried about the impending qualifying tests, because Maria told us we would do fine on those tests. She guaranteed it. "Trust me," she said. "You *will* pass."

When only 3 of 10 table leaders passed the first test, Maria remained confident. "I'm sure you'll do it on this one," she said of our second and final chance.

Maria proved prescient in that regard, although not necessarily due to our sudden brilliance. Caitlin was the first person to finish the second qualifying test, and after she handed her score sheet to Maria, Maria held up her hand to tell Caitlin not to move. After Maria checked the scores, she handed the score sheet back to Caitlin, whispered something to her, and sent her back to her desk, where Caitlin started to rescore the 10 essays. Then Maria whispered something to Ricky at her side, a something Ricky turned and whispered into the ear of the table leader closest to him.

The whispering continued through the room. Harlan, on my left, passed on to me the useful nugget: "The same score is never given to successive essays. Pass it on." Looking down at the score sheet in front of me, I saw I'd given the score of 2 to essays 1, 2, and 3, so I knew at least one of them was wrong. I turned to Pete on my right and repeated the information to him. He looked at his score sheet, nodded thankfully, and then repeated that same information to the table leader on his right. Like a game of Telephone, that hint was passed through the entire room.

A minute later the process was repeated, and Harlan relayed the news: "There's at least one of every score point in each qualifying set." Looking down at my score sheet, I saw I'd given no 1's, an oversight I'd have to remedy immediately. Then Maria passed to Ricky who passed to the table leaders the information that essay 2 "was *absolutely* considered appropriate five-paragraph format," meaning it would earn at least a 3. When Harlan whispered that to me, I knew my score of 2 was wrong, so I changed that incorrectly scored essay while hence solving my earlier problem of the repeated score of 2 on essays 1 through 3.

"And 10 is a 4," Harlan told me.

"Ten is a 4," I told Pete.

And so it was that Maria, our fearless leader, was correct: I *did* pass the qualifying test. We all did.

Our first assignment as table leaders was to look cool. Starting Monday morning, Maria would repeat the exact training to the 100 scorers she had just given to the 10 table leaders, and she wanted us supervisors to exude calm and confidence before the scorers had to take their own qualifying tests. She wanted us to keep the scorers from freaking out or arguing too vociferously with the training that would ensue, especially since we knew that training was likely going to be a fiasco. The training ended up being pretty funny, though, and we supervisors smirked as Maria squirmed: every complaint we table leaders had voiced was repeated by the scorers, and Maria had to defuse the situation repeatedly.

"No, turning in an outline won't earn the score of 3," she told them.

"Yes, Anchor #7 *is* a 2," she confirmed.

"No, formatting isn't the *only* thing we care about," she said.

"Yes, there probably will be a whole lot of 2's," she agreed.

That project was particularly problematic because it included both the usual subjectivity/ambiguity of scoring essays *and* the fact many of us simply disagreed with the way that state was meting out scores—using their rubric, we would have to give lower-half scores to some beautifully written student responses. The situation, however, would've been worse for the scorers if there weren't a whole lot of guarantees flying around the room that everyone *would* pass the qualifying tests. We supervisors promised the tests were a breeze, a fact that turned out to be true. All the scorers passed, aided by no more than a deluge of hints from us table leaders. Although Maria hadn't told us we should help the scorers pass their qualifying tests, it was pretty much understood: she said enough times that we couldn't afford to lose *any* of the 100 of them that her message was abundantly clear.

By Thursday morning, the training was done, everyone was "qualified," and it was time to score essays. At my table, under my supervision, I had 10 scorers, including Terry. While Terry was every bit as capable as I was of scoring tests, no one ever considered him for a promotion—the poor boy was barely able to manage himself, so no one expected he could supervise anyone else. The other scorers at my table were brand-new, however, including Erin and Wendy, two women in their early 20s. Louise was an older woman who was very quiet and very shy but who was beloved at our table because she regularly delivered us freshly baked cookies.

The most worrisome scorer at my table was a guy named Harry, a 50-ish fellow who showed up the first day wearing a plaid blazer, a short-sleeved dress shirt, and a clip-on tie. On his head Harry wore Buddy Holly glasses, circa 1958, and he had thick, black hair plastered down with gel, a huge part on the left side. He looked a bit like Pee Wee Herman (although he lacked Pee Wee's charm), and I got the feeling Harry was none too happy about his current situation. I understood why during the introductions, when Harry explained he'd recently lost his job at the refrigerator plant in Amana—"30 years wasted," he said. Although after the first day Harry never again wore a coat and tie (opting instead for T-shirts and a [John] Deere cap), he continued to wear a look of considerable disappointment. I got the feeling Harry might be the disgruntled type, and I was expecting every day when I read the newspaper to see some story about him shooting up his old workplace. I noted to myself not to tick Harry off.

When the scoring began, I wanted to be a good table leader, wanted to be liked by the people I supervised. I gave a little speech at my table in which I promised my scorers I would treat them like adults and promised I would *never*, for any reason, ask them why they'd been in the bathroom so long. I made it clear such things were beneath us all. I told them to use the phones when they wanted and take breaks when they needed, as long as they managed to score enough essays to meet our required goals. I wished them good luck and told them to get busy.

I made an effort to review the first packet that each of my 10 people completed, because I wanted to see how they were scoring, but it was difficult because I was getting swamped with questions and advice. Terry was always standing beside me, asking for my opinion about an essay he was reading, and Louise was meekly approaching every couple of minutes, with apologies each time, asking what she should do about this essay or that one. My other scorers came up with questions a little less frequently, but they did keep coming up, and Maria kept swinging by to make suggestions or comments ("Don't forget to fill out the time sheets"; "Remember, no parking in the Yen Ching lot"; "Get your people to sign their confidentiality agreements"). Meanwhile, the piles of completed packets and score sheets were accumulating higher on my desk—as many questions as Terry and Louise and the rest had, the 10 of them were also scoring and scoring, continuing to fill in bubbles as the clock ticked away.

To save time and keep them from bothering me, I eventually tried to convince both Terry and Louise they were absolute geniuses. Whenever they asked me what *I* thought an essay deserved, I asked them the same question.

"I'm not sure, Terry/Louise," I might say. "What do *you* think?"

If they were making a terribly obvious mistake, I might point it out to them, but if Terry/Louise were generally right about a score, I celebrated with them like they were little kids winning a prize. "Yes, Terry/Louise," I would say, "I think it's a 4 also! Great work! Keep it up!" After I'd done it enough times, both of them gained enough confidence they finally began to give me something of a break—they kept asking questions, but at least it was a little less regularly.

Nonetheless, the completed packets and score sheets kept piling up (in effect, 10 more essays were scored at my table every two minutes), and I never really got a chance to review anyone's scores on their own. Instead, I began to look at packets of essays that had been scored by two of my people, so I could review both of their scores simultaneously. I would find the completed score sheet of both the first scorer and the second scorer, and I would compare the results:

Packet #154 First Scorer: Erin		Packet #154 Second Scorer: Wendy	
Essay #1	2	Essay #1	3
Essay #2	2	Essay #2	2
Essay #3	4	Essay #3	4
Essay #4	2	Essay #4	2
Essay #5	3	Essay #5	3
Essay #6	2	Essay #6	2
Essay #7	3	Essay #7	2
Essay #8	2	Essay #8	2
Essay #9	3	Essay #9	3
Essay #10	2	Essay #10	2

With any luck, the scorers would agree with one another at least 70 percent of the time (like the 80 percent here), which was the required reliability for that project. As long as the agreement was 70 percent, I could place the packet in the "completed" pile and turn in the score sheets to be scanned. If the reliability was acceptable, I wouldn't even bother looking at the essays (I didn't have time), assuming my scorers had assessed them correctly. At that point I would also go back to each of those scorers to tell them I had reviewed their work and I thought they were doing a great job, a *great* job, a move I made regularly to both bolster the scorers' confidence and ensure that if I returned later, with complaints about their scoring, they wouldn't cry, hate my guts, or (in Harry's case) cut me down in a fusillade of bullets. I also made a point to regularly deliver doughnuts or bagels to my team, to keep their spirits up and to keep me from being reviled. Harlan, Greg, and Pete said those treats were making them look bad in front of *their* teams, but it was every man for himself on that project.

When the scorers didn't agree with each other to the tune of at least 70 percent reliability, however, I had problems:

Packet #177 First Scorer: Harry		Packet #177 Second Scorer: Louise	
Essay #1	2	Essay #1	3
Essay #2	3	Essay #2	2
Essay #3	2	Essay #3	3
Essay #4	2	Essay #4	2
Essay #5	4	Essay #5	4
Essay #6	2	Essay #6	2
Essay #7	1	Essay #7	1
Essay #8	2	Essay #8	3
Essay #9	2	Essay #9	3
Essay #10	3	Essay #10	3

If the agreement was poor (like the 50 percent here), it meant I would actually have to review the essays to see if either (or maybe both?) of my scorers was screwing up too obviously. I would review the responses where the scores didn't match (essays 1, 2, 3, 8, and 9 in this example) to see what the problem was. Sometimes an essay is right on the line between two score points, so arguing unequivocally that it is *absolutely* a 2 or a 3 is not possible; and if the scorers gave differing scores on an essay like that, I wouldn't even bother to discuss it with them. If, however, an essay was pretty clearly a 2 and some scorer gave it a 3, in those cases I would march over to the errant scorer and try to straighten him or her out. I wasn't doing it to be a know-it-all, but our lives would be so much easier if we could score in some sort of consistent, standardized way. I would kneel down next to the "wrong" scorer and have a little heart-to-heart chat. My speech always started the same, regardless of how well or how poorly I really thought the scorer was doing.

"Well, Louise," I might say, "you are doing a great job, a *great* job. I've been reviewing your work, and I almost always agree with you. But . . . ."

At that point, the scorer would nearly always tense up, awaiting the bad news.

"But," I would continue, "on the occasions I disagree with you, I think you are scoring too high. Look at this essay. . . ."

And I would hand her an essay on which her score disagreed with what the other scorer *and* I thought it really deserved.

"You gave this a 3," I might say, "but look at all the sentence fragments and run-on sentences." I actually had no idea if Louise knew what a sentence fragment or a run-on sentence was (I knew only that she baked a mean chocolate chip cookie), but I said it to her anyway. Even if she nodded at my comments, there wasn't necessarily any recognition in her eyes.

"The essay seems to lack proper paragraphing, too," I might add, "for the appropriate five-paragraph format." Again she would nod, but mostly she looked scared. "So, Louise, I think you're doing a great job, a *great* job, but when I disagree with you, I find you are usually scoring high."

She would nod enthusiastically at that, at something I think she finally understood, probably making a vow to herself to give lower scores. She might not know why she was doing it, but she could certainly give lower scores. "Don't drastically change your scoring," I would warn. "Basically keep doing what you're doing, but when you're hedging between a 2 and a 3 on some essay, maybe you should fall more frequently on the 2 side from now on."

She would earnestly agree, promising to do better, swearing she got it now. I wondered about that, before I marched over to the other scorer and repeated the entire process.

"Excuse me, Harry," I might say, holding my breath that he wouldn't start shooting before I got to my suck-up speech, "you are doing a great job, a *great* job. . . ." Then I would go through the whole rigmarole with Harry, telling him although I usually agreed with him, when I didn't it was because I thought he was scoring a little low.

"Look," I might say, "you're giving this essay a 2 even though it's perfectly formatted and has a great flow to it, great rhythm. It's very stylistic."

He would nod, as Louise had, but I wasn't sure if he understood, either, the formatting bit or the "stylistic" bit. The guy had been building refrigerators for 30 years, so I wasn't at all sure of his mastery of the literary elements. But because I wanted Harry to understand what I meant—both because I wanted my group to agree and because I didn't want to be in the danger zone of his desk again—I tried to explain myself without being too patronizing.

"Good word choices and vibrant language," I would say, pointing out examples of each to him, "sentences that vary from long to short, from simple to complex. . . ."

He would nod, maybe understanding and maybe not, and I would ask him to be a bit more generous when scoring before I fled back to the safety of my own desk. There I would look again at the scores Harry and Louise had given, and I would change a couple of them to represent the conversations I'd had with the two of them. Then I would dump the packet into the "completed" pile and turn in the score sheets to be scanned, it occurring to me as I did so that I had altered the reliability score for that packet from 50 percent up to 80 percent, making it look like Harry and Louise were scoring very consistently when they were obviously not. It worried me that maybe I was messing with the statistics, so I consulted with my fellow table leaders.

When I asked Caitlin (the supervisor who sat at the table on my right and who was working on her first project) what she was doing about the reliability numbers, she seemed amused. "I've got this eraser, you see," she smiled, "and when my scorers don't agree, I help them out."

"Really?" I asked.

"I didn't in the beginning," she said, "but since I can't get my scorers to actually agree, I had to do something. I make their scores match and turn in the sheets to be scanned. Pete told me what he was doing, so . . . ."

When I asked Harlan (who sat at the table on my left and who'd been a supervisor for years) the reliability question, he just laughed. "Of course you're changing them," he smiled. "How else would we get through this project?"

"Really?" I asked.

"Uh-huh." Then, like the Ghost of Reliabilities Doctored, Harlan took me on a short tour of the scoring center to show me what he meant. In the corner, Maria and Ricky were reading essays, but after they'd assessed and scored a packet, they simply copied the results onto the second score sheet, using Maria's ID number on one and Ricky's on the next, guaranteeing high "agreement" between the two of them even when the essays had only been read by one. That explained why Maria and Ricky's agreement statistics were always astronomically high, a result I had noticed when reviewing the daily reports.

Harlan showed me Greg at his desk, copying the exact same way, although he was using his own ID number and the ID number of whichever of his scorers had the lowest reliability, thus ensuring that scorer would eke out at least a 70 percent overall agreement and would be saved from a toothless "probation." That was a shortcut I ended up using with Harry—padding his stats by making scores given under his ID number match scores given under mine—if only to keep him from getting perturbed at his low reliability number and going postal on me. Watching Greg at his desk, I flashed back to my conversation with him from a couple of years before: "The reliability numbers are what we make them," he'd said.

Harlan and I were headed over to Pete's to see what he was up to statistically when we were stopped short. We watched Pete respond to a question from one of his people about an essay's score by taking the essay, holding it up to his head without even glancing at it (à la the Johnny Carson "mind-reading" bit from the *Tonight Show*), and announcing, "Carnac says this essay earns a 2." When his scorer began to debate that, Pete sent him away with a dismissive flick of the hand and a repeat of his earlier proclamation, "Carnac says it is a 2." Harlan and I just laughed. It seemed fairly certain Pete might be doctoring the statistics, too.

It got to be I had no other choice. The piles of scored packets kept growing higher on my desk; and even though I worked an hour of overtime each night, I still couldn't control the piles—I couldn't catch up. It was unmanageable, and expecting my scorers to *agree* was no more than a fantasy: A couple days after I'd talked to Louise and Harry about their differing scores, I reviewed another packet they'd both read and I found an unsettling result. Again Harry and Louise agreed with each other on only 50 percent of the essays, but this time Louise was scoring *low* and Harry was scoring *high*, the exact opposite of how they had scored the first packet. In my effort to get them to come to some middle ground, I had sent them rocketing right past each other to the other, far extreme.

I went through the same song and dance again, telling each of them, "You are doing a great job, a *great* job," before adding that caveat "but." This time I told Louise not to be so hard and I told Harry not to be so generous, and I showed a couple of examples of how both had screwed up. They each nodded their agreement to me before promising to get it right the next time.

The next time, however, when they were the first and second scorer of a third packet, although they managed to agree with each other on 60 percent of the essays (better, but still unacceptable), they had also overcorrected their scoring back to their original positions of Louise being too *high* and Harry being too *low*. I had to laugh, especially since that was happening with all my scorers—at some point they would score too high or too low, and then after my feedback they would dramatically overcorrect until they were erring to the other extreme.

One day I made an announcement. "OK, folks," I told them, "instead of coming around to you individually, I have this one bit of advice: those of you who are scoring too high, please score lower; and those of you who are scoring too low, please score higher. If you're scoring correctly, keep up the good work!"

They laughed, all except Terry, whose hand was in the air, surely to ask exactly where it was that he'd gone wrong. Eventually, given the ambiguity of the work—not to mention my dismay over giving out so many 2's to well-written essays—I began to forgo the visits to my scorers and just began to change their scores. If I saw that a scorer I trusted (Wendy, for instance) had disagreed with a scorer I didn't (Harry), I simply changed Harry's scores to match Wendy's: I erased the scores he had bubbled in and copied Wendy's. This ensured that our reliability would be acceptable, while also increasing the chance the student would get the correct score (which I imagined was Wendy's). I rarely, of course, actually looked at the essays in question, because I simply didn't have the time. If I was looking at the score sheets of two scorers I didn't trust (Louise and Harry, for example), eventually I compromised and erased bubbles from the score sheets of each, changing the scores until their agreement went from an unacceptable 50 or 60 percent up to an acceptable 70 percent. It was the only way I could ever get the packets off my desk and into the "completed" file.

What did all that cheating mean to the students and teachers of that state? I honestly don't know. I know only that I thought their scoring system was crazy to begin with (giving 2's to a number of masterpieces), but more important, I gave up on the idea you could get a huge group of people to consistently agree on the scores of all those essays. Opinions about writing have never been standardized (was *On The Road* one of the seminal books of the 20th century, as many argue, or was it no more than "typing," as Truman Capote said?), but expecting people to come to a consensus in a two-minute time frame, with a rubric like *that*? I didn't think so. So because I was unable to legitimately establish any "standardized" scoring system with my team, I simply fudged the statistics. The eraser was my only friend.

Ultimately, the manipulation of the reliability statistics wasn't the real tragedy of that writing assessment. That occurred halfway through the project when the holier-than-thou Roseanne returned to Iowa City, where she discovered—exactly as had been predicted—that her rubric was producing an astounding number of 2's. In fact, nearly 70 percent of all the scores we had given were 2's, a number Roseanne viewed with horror.

"There are 67 percent 2's!" she screamed in Maria's office. "Oh, my God!"

That number was troubling on two fronts. First, that many 2's indicated a lot of failing students and failing schools in Roseanne's state, and, second, the number verged on being statistically invalid. If everyone got a 2, what did a 2 mean? How would the state know whom to give bonuses to if everyone was no good?

Roseanne bemoaned her fate, whining and complaining about the situation, but ultimately she came up with a simple solution. "Give more 3's," she told Maria to tell us. "Just give more 3's."

Roseanne didn't tell Maria to use a different rubric. She didn't tell her to start the whole process over. She didn't indicate anything could be done about the essays that had already been scored. Roseanne simply told Maria, who told us table leaders, who told the scorers, to "give more 3's." Although we couldn't actually change the scores of any training papers (because that would indicate the process wasn't completely "standardized"), Roseanne did say we should start thinking about an essay like Anchor Paper #7 as a 3, not a 2. That should help the numbers, she said.

What a surprise! Anchor Paper #7 *wasn't* a 2! While we table leaders and scorers may have wanted to laugh and be smug about having been proven correct, it was too depressing to do so: the kids were getting screwed now. Even if we table leaders had been doctoring the reliability statistics, at least the essays were being read and scored by people giving an honest assessment as to an essay's ability based on that state's rubric. And even if many of us didn't agree with the rubric, the scorers in that room, to the best of their abilities, still followed its tenets and doled out the scores based on its parameters. Our scoring may have been inconsistent, but it was at least theoretically fair.

Roseanne's solution was something else entirely. When she didn't like the results of her test, she simply changed the way we would score them, ensuring she got the numbers she wanted. We were all aghast at her decision, including Maria, but Maria—the only full-time NCS employee in that entire room of more than 100 people—reminded us of one important point: the customer was always right. If Roseanne wanted to change the way we'd been scoring—standardization be damned!—then change it we would. We would give more 3's, which is what we did. By the end of the project, the number of 2's had been reduced to a much more reasonable 50 percent of all the scores, just as Roseanne had asked.

I realize how hypocritical it might be for me—the Man with the Omnipotent Eraser—to complain about what Roseanne had done, but there seems to me a considerable difference between a temporary employee taking shortcuts and a government employee supposedly dedicated to helping her students basically throwing half of those kids under the train. Per Roseanne's instructions, essays of *exactly the same ability* would get different scores based only on *when* they were read: essays that would have earned a 2 in the first half of the project would earn a 3 during the second half, and on an assessment that *mattered*! It was a little bit sickening to think about, but Roseanne didn't seem too troubled by her decision; and after she made it, she flew blithely back to her state capital, leaving in her wake nothing but a building full of disillusioned test scorers and the essays of her doomed students.

I'd like to say that was the last I ever saw of Roseanne in the world of testing, but I'm afraid it's not true. While the good news may be that Roseanne no longer works for any state department of education, the bad news is now she works for a testing company. A *for-profit* testing company.

I shudder to think of the malfeasances she currently manages. If Roseanne couldn't do the right thing in a job where *children* were supposed to be her first priority, I can't imagine what she's capable of when all she answers to is the bottom line.

The Oracle of Princeton

NOTWITHSTANDING the ethical lapses I suffered from or the sacrifice of students I was witness to, my first supervisory work on that writing assessment was a personal success. Maria searched me out afterward to ask what the hell I'd done to the people on my team: the evaluations my scorers had written about me were absolutely glowing.

"Did you threaten them?" she laughed. "Bribe them?"

"Nothing in particular," I smiled, realizing my barrage of daily compliments and regular breakfast pastries had paid off. "Just doing my job."

"Wow," Maria said, fanning out the 10 evaluations in front of her. "These people adore you."

"Oh, well," I said, all faux humility. "They were just nice people, I think."

Maria was scanning the evaluations. "'Todd is 'very help-ful,'" she read. "He's 'supportive,' 'smart,' 'charming.' There's not a negative comment about you."

"They're too kind," I said, "too kind." I pretended I couldn't imagine getting such high praise, but in my head I was beaming, those fawning reviews of my managerial style—nay, of my very *essence*—confirming my long-held belief that I was extraordinary.

Maria continued reading to herself, shaking her head with disbelief. "I've never seen such evaluations," she said, and before she walked away, she patted my arm. "Great job, Todd." I was proud I'd had such an effect on my scorers and happy to have made such a favorable impression on Maria.

Those flattering reviews occurred at just the right time, because by the spring of '98, the testing business was booming, and NCS was beginning to open scoring centers all across America. They would need experienced supervisors to travel to other states to oversee projects, and when Maria thought about whom to send, my name was near the top of her list.

Finally I was getting somewhere, because even if my efforts to get into the Writers' Workshop hadn't exactly panned out (a tactful rejection letter having landed in my mailbox that very spring), traveling for NCS meant two things: *four* more dollars an hour, and living on an expense account. Ka-ching!

My first jaunt on the NCS dime was to one of Iowa's neighboring states, where Harlan and I headed to do range-finding work on that state's reading test. Harlan swung by my apartment on Brown Street to pick me up, because we were taking his car on the long trek north.

"Why is it we are *driving*?" I asked him.

"Thirty-three cents a mile," Harlan told me, explaining that was how much he could charge on his expense account for the use of a personal vehicle. "It's more than 600 miles up and back," he smiled. "Do the math."

"Nice," I said.

"Plus," he added, "we're about to get paid 14 bucks an hour to spend two full days commuting to and from the capital, aren't we?"

"You are a wise man," I said, computing in my head 16 hours times $14, minus 25 percent of the gross to taxes . . . .

Range finding turned out to be very different from scoring. When working on a scoring project—whether as a scorer or a table leader—the only thing to do was learn a system someone else had established and then apply that system when assessing the student responses. Even if you didn't agree with the system (like the reading rubric that credited posters that included myriad *bad* bike safety rules, or the unduly harsh focused-holistic writing rubric we had just been using), you couldn't ignore it— you simply had to follow its rules, happily or not, doling out the points exactly as it said. There may have been a little leeway in interpreting those rules, but the rules themselves didn't change.

Range finding wasn't about following the rules at all. Range finding was about coming up with the rules, establishing a system to score each item that would later be followed by all those lowly NCS peons. At range finding, an NCS representative would meet with a small group of a state's teachers to work out how they wanted to give out the points on their test (the state test we were about to work on had been piloted the year before, so we would hopefully be confirming the last year's decisions were sound). It sounded to me like an interesting mental exercise where my opinion would finally matter, certainly a better gig than mindlessly scoring, but Harlan told me not to get too excited.

"Get ready to kiss some ass," he said. Harlan explained that while the state educators were almost always nice people, they also thought their experience as teachers made them the only experts, meaning quite clearly we testing people were not.

"You'll hear a number of times," he said, "'I've been a teacher for 27 years,' . . . 'for 18 years,' . . . 'for 31 years.'"

"Yeah," I told him, "well, I coached JV soccer one fall."

"Oh, be sure to tell them that," he nodded.

"Before I got fired for swearing," I continued.

"Yeah, definitely tell them," he said.

We would be in the state capital for two days. Harlan would be leading a group of teachers on the seventh-grade range finding, while I would lead a group on the fourth grade. Both groups would work together on one of my items the first morning, to establish how the procedure worked. Harlan told me the most important thing about the process was to survive it.

"There might be a lot of complaints," he said. "This group might hate our items and rubrics, even though they were all pilot-tested last year." They might even hate us, Harlan kidded, but he explained we needed to do whatever necessary to get through the two days and end up with the committees' approval on our work. Harlan said then when it was time to actually score the student responses in Tucson in March, we could—far from the reach of any of those teachers—do whatever the hell we wanted with all those items and rubrics.

"Nice," I said. "But is that how range finding is *supposed* to go?"

"It's the only way it can," he told me. "Imagine letting 10 teachers try to come up with a scoring system on their own. They would come up with something much too complex, not understanding what really happens at a scoring center."

After the long drive north, we checked into an Embassy Suites in the capital city's downtown. I had assumed we would be sharing a hotel room, but Harlan rolled his eyes at that. "Please," he said, "get your own." Sure enough, a room had been reserved in my name, too (and prepaid, at that), but when we moved in, I wondered why. My suite, exactly like Harlan's, had a bedroom with two queen beds, plus a sofa bed in the living room—it could sleep at least six people. I asked Harlan about all that wasted space, and he shrugged.

"Not my money," he said.

The next morning we went to work, me and Harlan from NCS, one representative of the state Department of Education, and a group of 12 teachers. We made introductions, shared some pleasantries, and nibbled from the food trays before we began. The item we first worked on was from the fourth-grade test, a four-point reading comprehension question. Students read an article about the taste buds and were instructed to answer a number of questions about it, including "Name your favorite food and identify its flavor. Explain where on your tongue and how you taste it."

There wasn't necessarily supposed to be any discussion about the *item*. Since it had already been administered to the state's fourth graders on the January test, complaining about the question itself seemed like an exercise in futility. That, however, didn't stop the range-finding committee from bitching.

A middle-aged, red-haired woman wearing a Christmas sweater spoke first, and though she reminded me of Mrs. Claus, she didn't look very jolly. "What a terrible item," she said. "Who wrote this?"

"Just atrocious," an elderly white-haired lady added. "You can't ask a child about his favorite food and then expect him to explain the taste buds. He'll lose focus."

"Terrible," another tsk-tsked. "Who wrote this item?"

I was a little surprised, because I thought we were discussing the *scoring* of the items, the way we would hand out points for the student responses. I looked at Harlan, hoping he had an answer for the perturbed educators, because I had nothing to tell this fire-breathing bunch about the actual test questions.

"NCS does not write the items," Harlan said, "but I do know that process also includes your state's educators. Along with a test development company, the items are written by local teachers."

"Really?" a younger male member of the committee replied, shaking his head. "I don't know what they were thinking." His dismay was echoed by the remaining educators in the room, that group of teachers utterly aghast at what a previous group of educators had once done.

It was no different with the rubrics. Our range-finding committee believed the rubrics were also fatally flawed. Their shortcomings became abundantly obvious as soon as we saw the one for that first taste bud question:

Reading Comprehension
Grade 4

4 The student response includes all four of the following elements:
It identifies a favorite food.
It describes that food's flavor as sweet, sour, salty or bitter.
It identifies where on the tongue that flavor can be found (correct answers should say sweet and salty are on the front of tongue, sour on the side, and bitter in the back).
It explains tastes are experienced either on the "taste buds" or the "papillae."

3 The student response includes three of the four elements above.
2 The student response includes two of the four elements above.
1 The student response includes one of the four elements above.
0 The student response includes none of the four elements above.

"The students get a point for identifying their favorite food?" Mrs. Claus scoffed. "How is that reading comprehension?" She shook her head as the other teachers nodded in agreement.

Harlan answered. "Last year we thought—"

The white-haired woman interrupted him, her words as harsh as a ruler across the knuckles. "Excuse me," she spit out, "this is *our* test."

Harlan conceded immediately, "I know."

The unjolly Mrs. Claus continued, "They get another point for saying 'taste buds'?" she asked. "A point for saying 'taste buds help you taste'?" She was incredulous. They all were.

"Who wrote this rubric?" Mrs. Claus asked.

Harlan prepared to reply, looking first at the teacher who'd rebuked him to be sure she'd allow him to talk. Since she, too, seemed to be awaiting the answer, Harlan said, "The rubric was written by last year's range-finding committee of your state's teachers in this very hotel."

"No!" Mrs. Claus exclaimed. "I can't believe that." She shook her head as if it were impossible, as if Harlan were literally lying to her. It took the confirmation of Gwen, the Department of Education woman, to convince the teachers we NCS bastards weren't solely responsible for what they perceived as this terrible rubric. Gwen promised that state teachers had definitely been involved last year in writing it.

"What were they *thinking*?" Mrs. Claus said. "I've been a teacher for 21 years, and I've never seen anything like this."

I had to stifle a smile. It was even harder when the white-haired woman played her trump card.

"I've been a teacher for *31* years," she said haughtily, and even if she was agreeing with Mrs. Claus, she'd also put her in her place. "And I wonder the same thing. *What were they thinking?*"

It was a question repeated for the next two days, regarding about half the items and rubrics in the fourth-grade group and half the items and rubrics in the seventh-grade group: "*What were they thinking?*" The committees Harlan and I were working with were pretty much convinced those former committees had been out of their friggin' minds.

The only way Harlan and I managed to survive the two days of range finding was by showing the teachers carefully selected student responses that confirmed the efficacy of the items and rubrics in their existing states. We had spent the previous week in Iowa City looking at hundreds of student responses from the January administration of the test, so we brought with us examples of student responses that showed the items and rubrics working beautifully. In the case of my first taste bud item, that meant I showed the committee examples of excellent answers getting excellent scores and poor answers getting poor scores.

I happily showed the range-finding committee a complete and well-written student response that earned the score of 4 on the existing rubric, the very result any self-respecting elementary teacher would want it to earn:

> Name your favorite food and identify its flavor. Explain where on your tongue and how you taste it.
> *My favorite food is ice cream, which is very sweet. The flavor of sweet is found on the tip of the tongue (as is salty). Taste is experienced when the food touches the papillae.*

Then I showed the range-finding committee a bad answer, a brief and butchered response that earned the lowest score of 1 on our rubric (for identifying a favorite food only), a result any teacher would have a hard time disputing:

> Name your favorite food and identify its flavor. Explain where on your tongue and how you taste it.
> *Candy is delishus I love it in my mouth and put as much in as I can at once time.*

I showed the committee dozens of papers, good answers getting good scores and bad answers getting bad ones, all of them confirming the effectiveness of the item and rubric. I pretended I hadn't seen, back in Iowa City, an endless array of weird responses getting bizarre and maybe inappropriate scores. I didn't tell the committee about the four-word response that earned the score of 4:

> Name your favorite food and identify its flavor. Explain where on your tongue and how you taste it.
> *Chocolate   sweet   front   papillae*

I didn't tell them about the response that showed a nearly comprehensive understanding of the workings of the taste buds—the very purpose of the article the students had read!—that earned only the score of 1 (because it didn't identify a favorite food or its taste):

> Name your favorite food and identify its flavor. Explain where on your tongue and how you taste it.
> *When something tasty enters the mouth, its chemecals are disolved by the saliva, and the floating pieces enter the taste bud through a hole in it's center. If the moleculs sticks to the tip of a cell, it will tell that cell into sending a series of chemical and electrical signals.*

I didn't tell the committee about the huge number of responses claiming bizarre favorite foods ("I like to eat rocks"), didn't tell them about the many students listing the ingredients of their favorite foods ("Pizza is made with bread and cheese") or simply providing recipes to make them ("To make microwave popcorn you put it in a bowl"). To do so would only have led to more questions and complaints, and because Harlan and I both needed our respective committees to OK seven items over the course of two days, we figured what the committees didn't know wouldn't hurt them. It certainly wouldn't hurt us to keep them in the dark, so we only showed them examples that proved the value of our items and rubrics.

Because my committee's entire context for understanding the items and rubrics resulted only from the student responses I showed them, pretty soon those teachers began to sign off on my work. Eventually, for each of my items, the committee conceded, shelving any complaints they may have had and ultimately giving their endorsements. That was good news, because it meant the Department of Education could honestly claim the work was approved by its state's classroom teachers, and it also allowed Harlan and me to escape to Iowa City.

We didn't escape immediately, however. While our NCS project manager had wanted us to drive back after the second day of range finding, Harlan and I didn't think so: we weren't making any six-hour drive after an eight-hour day. Instead, with no one's permission, Harlan and I simply extended our stays at the Embassy Suites (it wasn't our money) to enjoy a night on the town. At the hotel's "Manager Reception," we enjoyed a quick cocktail to take the edge off, but when the reception ended, Harlan and I jumped in his car and headed off on an ill-advised quest for a steak house. Not knowing where we were going, we circled the state capital, hoping to magically stumble on some old-school restaurant serving up big slabs of red meat and tall glasses of red wine. In our pursuit we crossed bridges (from one side of the mighty Mississippi River to the other), drove through tunnels, and rode on side streets and superhighways, not finding what we were looking for but unwilling to give up. We drove and drove.

At some point, I noticed the capital fading into our rear-view mirror, and I had to suggest to Harlan that we might want to head back toward the bright lights of the big city. A bit later, after an illegal U-turn or two, we made our way back to the city before it again started to fade into the rear view, and I had to point out to Harlan that we seemed then to be speeding toward Chicago. Eventually we did make it safely back to the capital, and in search of our Holy Grail, we drove around in circles, absolutely refusing to give up while dreaming of a porterhouse, medium-rare.

Unfortunately, we never found that oasis and ate no steak that night, but at some point during our search I did have an epiphany. I realized our quest for a steak house was a bit like scoring essays: first we went too far one way, then too far the other, and ultimately we just ended up in the middle, lost and confused.

The first time I flew for NCS was the week after Harlan and I returned from the reading range-finding meeting, when I jetted off to Princeton to work with the bigwigs at Educational Testing Service (ETS) doing range finding for the 1998 NAEP writing assessment. NAEP (also known as the "Nation's Report Card") is considered the "gold standard" of standardized testing, an assessment funded by the U.S. government to evaluate where the country's students stand in certain subject areas, and to have been selected by Maria as one of the NCS trainers was quite a coup for me. None of my male friends made the cut, so instead I headed off to New Jersey that February with Caitlin and a gaggle of women I'd never worked with before.

We were led by Celia, a very nice and very efficient woman who was all about dotting *i*'s and crossing *t*'s, the mother hen type who spent all her time trying to keep us in line, a task she had more luck with at work than away from it. My friend Caitlin was there, and while Caitlin was sweet, she was also trying to seduce me, an offer I found problematic due to her red-necked, pickup-driving, rifle-toting husband back in Iowa. Missy was a married woman who spent a lot of her time in Princeton at the hotel bar, either chasing or being chased by some English bloke from California, the two of them not quite able to decide whether to go down the path of adultery. The other two NCS staff were Stephanie and Maureen, women who spent their downtime in Princeton at the Yankee Doodle Tap room ordering a steady supply of the bar's garlic mashed potatoes, the two of them lasciviously eyeing and eventually chowing down on steaming pile after steaming pile of spuds served in charming pewter pots.

Although those Iowans may not have been my ideal choice for traveling companions, I didn't doubt their qualifications for the work. Each of those women had advanced degrees or teaching experience, a couple of résumé fillers I certainly could not claim. In fact, I was a little worried I might not even get through the doors of the ETS offices, at least not if they did any background check and looked up my SAT score.

NAEP range finding would be a little different from the semi-fraud I had just perpetrated on the last state's teachers, because for NAEP everyone would be looking at the student responses for the first time. There'd been no chance for us to prep the essays in advance, so in Princeton we would all—ETS staff, NCS staff, and random national writing experts—review student responses together and try to establish some sort of standardized scoring system.

The NAEP writing range finding was on ETS's sprawling Princeton campus, and it was led by the charming Clarice, a feisty woman wearing an Ann Taylor ensemble, a little woman with a big laugh and a quick mind who called herself a "Princeton matron" and seemed to revel in that description. I was glad Clarice seemed so nice, because I was otherwise cowed by everything I saw. Clarice's introductory speech included all kinds of subjects I'd never heard of ("items maps," "achievement levels," "writing framework"), and the roughly 30 people in the room were an intimidating lot. The ETS group looked about as I had expected—the men clad in various conservative combinations of tweeds and sweater vests, the women all donning sensible shoes—but they wowed me with their credentials, an endless collection of Ivy League educations and PhDs. The outside consultants were even more imposing, academic deans and university department heads who were national leaders in writing education. As everyone listed their qualifications, I slunk lower and lower in my chair—while the rest of them had fat résumés and numerous sheepskins, I had ended up in that room largely because I had charmed Maria back in Iowa City. When introducing myself, I alluded to some murky graduate school past and tried to impress the group with the breadth and depth of my experience on writing assessments (I didn't mention the skimming and scoring part of reading essays), and when I was done, Clarice smiled at me and moved on.

To begin the project, we would work together on one writing item as a whole to really hammer things out, to fully and firmly establish exactly how we would mete out points for that assessment. It was our one chance to set up a clear, consistent, and standardized scoring system before we broke into smaller groups.

The item we worked on as a big group was a descriptive question, a fourth-grade prompt that instructed the students to write about a favorite thing.

1998 NAEP Writing Assessment
Grade 4 Descriptive

We all have favorite objects that we care about and would not want to give up.

Think of one object that is important or valuable to you. For example, it could be a book, a piece of clothing, a game, or any object you care about.

Write about your favorite object. Be sure to describe the object and explain why it is valuable or important to you.

Source: From the NAEP Web site at http://nces.ed.gov/nationsreportcard/ITMRLS/itemdisplay.asp.

The rubric we would use was tried and tested, a six-point scoring guide that had been a part of the NAEP assessment for years. It went from the high of "excellent" to the low of "unsatisfactory," a number between 6 and 1 equating to each descriptor.

Six-Point Scoring Guide

Excellent
- Develops ideas well and uses specific, relevant details across the response.
- Is well organized with clear transitions.
- Sustains varied sentence structure and exhibits specific word choices.
- Exhibits control over sentence boundaries; errors in grammar, spelling, and mechanics do not interfere with understanding.

Skillful
- Develops ideas with some specific, relevant details.
- Is clearly organized; information is presented in an orderly way, but response may lack transitions.
- Exhibits some variety in sentence structure and exhibits some specific word choices.
- Generally exhibits control over sentence boundaries; errors in grammar, spelling, and mechanics do not interfere with understanding.

Sufficient
- Clear but sparsely developed; may have few details.
- Provides a clear sequence of information; provides pieces of information that are generally related to each other.

- Generally has simple sentences and simple word choice; may exhibit uneven control over sentence boundaries.
- Has sentences that consist mostly of complete, clear, distinct thoughts; errors in grammar, spelling, and mechanics generally do not interfere with understanding.

Uneven
- May be characterized by one or more of the following:
- Provides limited or incomplete information; may be list-like or have the quality of an outline.
- Is disorganized or provides a disjointed sequence of information.
- Exhibits uneven control over sentence boundaries and may have some inaccurate word choices.
- Errors in grammar, spelling, and mechanics sometimes interfere with understanding.

Insufficient
- May be characterized by one or more of the following:
- Provides little information and makes little attempt at development.
- Is very disorganized OR too brief for reader to detect organization.
- Exhibits little control over sentence boundaries and sentence formation; word choice is inaccurate in much of the response.
- Characterized by misspellings, missing words, incorrect word order; errors in grammar, spelling, and mechanics are severe enough to make understanding very difficult in much of the response.

Unsatisfactory
- May be characterized by one or more of the following:
- Attempts a response, but may only paraphrase the prompt or be extremely brief.
- Exhibits no control over organization.
- Exhibits no control over sentence formation; word choice is inaccurate across the response.
- Characterized by misspellings, missing words, incorrect word order; errors in grammar, spelling, and mechanics severely impede understanding across the response.

Source: From the NAEP Web site at http://nces.ed.gov/nationsreportcard/ITMRLS/itemdisplay.asp.

Frankly, I was looking forward to NAEP range finding because I wanted to see all those experts at work. I was hoping for some enlightenment from them, figuring that all the foolishness I'd been party to on other writing assessments would now be trumped on the NAEP project, it the finest test in all the land.

Or not.

If I'd always found it ridiculous to expect a large group of low-paid and maybe underqualified test scorers to come to any consensus about the quality of student writing, imagine getting a bunch of national writing experts to agree. With the NCS scorers, the trainer could simply say, "This response earns a 4 because the committee says so," which was an argument that couldn't be debated—the scorers *had* to concede, because their job was simply to follow directions. At NAEP writing range finding, however, it was all about opinions, and you couldn't tell any of those folks they were wrong. Because they were the leading lights in their field, those experts would grab hold of a position and never let go, their pedigrees convincing them of the utter brilliance of their stands, and they would hold on to those opinions in the face of any and all debate.

Our range finding, in other words, went rather slowly.

A response like the one below would end up causing a good hour's worth of deliberation.

1998 NAEP Writing Assessment
Grade 4 Descriptive

Write about your favorite object. Be sure to describe the object and explain why it is valuable or important to you.

The most valuable object to me is my teddy bear. I had that every sense I was five years old. Every day when I get some free time I go in my big room and start playing with her. It is so importent to me because my great great grandma gave it to my moma then my moma passed it o me. I play with it almost every day. I cary it every where I go. But my mother would never let me bring it to school. Because she thinks I'm going to let some one hold it and drop it in the mud. I know it is a teddy bear. I even take it a bath. I love that teddy bear with all my heart. I would never give me teddy bear up. I would never let it out of my sight. One day my sister was playing with my teddy bear. She was throwing it up and the air and caughting it. Then she heard the phone ring she dropped my cute little teddy bear she said I am going out side. She played outside for along time. She came back in the house at 6:00 o'clock. Her shoes was all muddy. She walked in her room tracking muddy foot steps. My teddy bear was on the floor. I walked tors her room I yelled out "NO." My sister said what. I jumed over all that junck and reached for my teddy bear I got their in time. Me and my teddy bear lived happy ever after.

Source: From the NAEP Web site at http://nces.ed.gov/nationsreportcard/ ITMRLS/itemdisplay.asp.

"Skillful?" One disbelieving writing expert would ask another. "You are saying we should see this as a 'skillful' response?"

"Well," the challenged might reply, massaging his bearded chin, "I do believe for a fourth-grade student doing on-demand writing, yes, this response is 'skillful.' I assume you don't agree?"

"I do not agree," the first might say. "I can't be party to such a generous assessment. While I realize the child is young, to overlook the obvious faults on the sentence level is, in my opinion, a mistake. In my most forgiving mood, I would only call this a 'sufficient' essay."

" 'Sufficient'!" someone else would cry, usually a former elementary teacher. "Have you ever seen a fourth-grade class-room? This writing, excluding the occasional error, is absolutely wonderful, full of descriptive details that explain the teddy bear's worth to the student. I'd call this an 'excellent' response for a fourth grader."

"Poppycock!" someone would yell, before the debate took off in some other direction. It was only through Clarice's deft handling of the group, and her tendency to make us vote on an essay's final score, that we actually managed to come to any consensus—not everyone agreed with every score, but Clarice went with majority rule. During all those debates, I kept my mouth firmly shut, understanding quite clearly my presence in that room was hanging by a thread. For me to pretend I was an expert in the field of writing education—or writing or edu-cation, for that matter—wasn't a risk I was willing to take.

It was only when I became completely exasperated that I finally spoke, when one brief essay evoked such a confused and contentious debate I couldn't keep my mouth shut any longer. Today I can no longer remember the essay exactly (it was too damned short to have any effect on my brain), but it roughly said:

Although not the obvious choice, like my house or family,
the object most important to me is one you might not
expect. It is my dog.

For maybe 30 minutes they argued about that essay, all two
and a half lines of it. One expert refused to call it a 1 because it
didn't lack "control" and didn't include "inaccurate" word
choices, descriptors on the rubric for the "unsatisfactory" score.
Another argued it had to be a 1 because it was "extremely
brief," like the rubric said, and while a third conceded that
point, she noted in terms of grammar and sentence construc-
tion the response was more closely linked to *upper-half* scores,
at least "generally exhibiting control" as opposed to "interfer-
ing" or "impeding" understanding. Another agreed the essay
had some upper-half qualities, commenting on its "sentence
variety." Back and forth they went, quoting different parts of
the rubric to each other, no one getting in the last word. Meanwhile, at my desk, I sat stunned. It was an essay I, and everyone
I knew at NCS, would have scored a 1 from five feet away. I
would have scored it a 1 if reading it while standing on my head,
would have scored it a 1 if it'd been written in a foreign tongue.

"Don't do it," I told myself. "Don't say a word!"

For a while I managed to keep quiet, but as more people
began to join the discussion, the more annoyed I became. It
was when one of them commented admiringly on the complex-
ity of the essay's first sentence I finally snapped. Like any good
New Englander, I'd kept my mouth shut and my feelings all
bottled up, so when I finally did speak, I nearly exploded.

"Are you all serious?" I demanded. "Are we really having
this debate?"

They all looked at me, suddenly quiet and a bit scared.
Who was I, again, they wondered?

"Yes, it's a well-constructed, complex sentence," I said.
"But it's a *sentence*! It is *one* of *two* sentences in this entire essay!

Clarice laughed at my outburst, which made me calm down a bit.

"This student has written 25 words!"

"Well," one of the nationally renowned writing experts began to instruct me, "length is *never* supposed to be a consideration."

I knew that very well. If there's one thing emphasized by everyone in the world of testing, it's that the length of an essay is not supposed to count toward its score. That was a sacred cow. Personally, I'd always wondered how any student writer was supposed to develop ideas without, you know, writing words; I'd always wondered how they were supposed to "exhibit sentence variety" without at least having more than a couple of sentences. But what did I know? I'd barely gone to graduate school.

"I understand," I said. "But how long do these students get to write?"

"Twenty-five minutes," Clarice said.

"So this student's written 25 words in 25 minutes, a word a minute. I'm supposed to think he was being *very* particular about each word? I'm supposed to think if we gave him another hour we might expect another 60 sophisticated words in a couple more complex sentences?"

No one said anything, although Clarice continued to look amused.

"This student has barely responded to this prompt," I said, "and to give him any score other than 1 is to overlook his refusal. This kid is clearly a good writer, maybe a great writer for fourth grade, but he's not given us an essay. He's given us two sentences."

With that I was done. I pushed back from the table and held up my hands.

A couple of seconds later Clarice spoke. "Of course, he's right," she said, and eventually everyone in the room agreed with her assessment of my outburst. Some agreed begrudgingly, but they all agreed. After 30 minutes' worth of heated debate about 25 fourth-grade words, we gave the response the score of 1 and moved on.

After two days of group scoring, when we had begun to come to some general agreement about how to score the essays (including incorporating my assertion that length matters at least somewhat when doling out points), we began to do the range-finding work on our individual items. In groups of two we scored for the rest of the week, occasionally checking with other teams or Clarice to confirm the accuracy of our work, and we began to select papers that would ultimately be used in the training sets. At the end of the day on Friday, we turned in all the essays we had scored so Clarice and her people could have a look.

When we adjourned again back at the ETS campus on Monday morning, Clarice brought everyone together in the conference room and made an announcement. "I have some bad news," she said. "It seems we haven't been scoring correctly."

There was a buzz in the room, both a disappointment we might've erred and a disbelief anyone could doubt *us*, the country's preeminent experts in the scoring of writing assessments. It was the most standardized our big group had ever been, a complete consensus that someone had some nerve to quibble with us.

"Says who?" a bespectacled fellow asked Clarice.

"Well," she replied, "our numbers don't match up with what the psychometricians predicted."

Grumblings from around the room followed, but I'd never heard the word before.

"The who?" I asked.

"The psychometricians," she said. "The stats people."

"What, they read the essays this weekend?" I asked.

Clarice laughed. "No," she said. "They read their spread-sheets."

"So?" I didn't mean to be a dunce, but I didn't get what was going on.

"They predicted we'd see between 6 and 9 percent 1's, but from the work we did last week, we're only seeing 3 percent. The rest of the numbers are pretty much on, but we're a little high on 2's and mostly short on 1's."

The sentence hung there, and no one said a word. I still didn't know what it really meant.

"They need us," Clarice explained, "to find more 1's."

Then I got it. I'm not a complete idiot. Generally, my colleagues seemed a little annoyed, but no one complained particularly. They seemed to settle into the fact they had more work to do: now we'd have to rescore the items we'd done the last week, as well as score the rest of the items we hadn't yet started. People seemed to want to buckle down and get to it. Time was a-wastin'.

Since I was new to the process—both to range finding and to NAEP—I assumed that's how things went. Because no one else made a big fuss about Clarice's announcement, I didn't, either. I began to rescore my items, searching for 1's in the pile of essays I'd already given other scores. Basically that meant I had to override the decisions about scoring made by the group of national writing experts the week before, but who was I to dissent? I assumed if the psychometricians could tell, without actually looking at the student responses, there should be more 1's, I figured there should be more 1's.

And because I had no choice in the matter, I found more 1's. I found 1's I thought were pretty clearly 2's, and I found 1's I thought should certainly be called "off task." If, however, the omniscient psychometricians wanted 1's, I'd give them 1's. My entire experience in the world of testing had taught me to be agreeable, so agreeable I was.

Ultimately, everyone found the necessary numbers, and eventually we each put together training sets that included 6 to 9 percent 1's. Those training sets were then used to teach the scorers how to assess the essays, and by the next year, when the 1998 NAEP writing statistics were released, I was amazed to see that the total number of 1's given on that year's test fell exactly between 6 and 9 percent.

Wow, I thought, what a bunch of Nostradamuses those psychometricians were. Absolutely friggin' brilliant.

The King of Scoring

BACK AT THE first range-finding meeting I attended, Harlan and I hadn't pulled the wool over the eyes of those teachers for the fun of it. We pulled the wool over their eyes because it was the only way to get the work done. While those teachers may have been experts in the classroom, Harlan and I were experts at the scoring center, and the two weren't necessarily related. Expecting classroom teachers to know how to differentiate between score points on a standardized test was as foolish an idea as leaving me in charge of a room full of fourth graders. It was the difference between teaching 20 students and testing 60,000.

Once I sat through a range-finding session with a bunch of classroom teachers who were writing the rubric for a dichotomous item (a correct answer would earn a 1, an incorrect answer a 0). The teachers asserted quite confidently that "Holly" was the correct answer to the question "Who is telling this story?" (a first-person narrative about a girl's family). The teachers told me quite assuredly that not only was "Holly" the correct answer, but it was the *only* correct answer. When I asked if they wanted to expand the rubric, the teachers snickered at me rather pedantically, silly-little-man-with-no-teaching-experience that I was. I should write "Holly" down on my little rubric, they told me, and then I should score the responses exactly like that.

Very good, I told them. The customer is always right.

Then two months later, in a distant state, when it was time to score that item, I expanded the rubric myself. It was the only fair thing to do. The first student response replied to the question "Who is telling this story?" with the answer "I." Given that "I" absolutely was the person telling the story, I accepted it. The second response said "The narrator," an even better answer I also credited. The third said "The person doing all the talking," and what's that but a way of saying "narrator" when you don't know the word? I accepted it. The fourth said "The daughter," and because Holly was the daughter in the story, I credited that, too. The fifth said "The sister," and ditto—that was good. I think I scored the first 15 papers without ever finding the answer "Holly," but every one of them still got credit. The teachers had been right, of course, and "Holly" was a correct answer, but it wasn't the *only* one. Not even close.

That disparity—between how any teacher/sane person might reasonably expect 20 students to reply to a question and the way 60,000 of them actually do—occurred on virtually every item I ever worked on, but never so clearly as on that first taste bud question. Scoring those student responses in Tucson that March, I saw how rubrics evolved, and it was an amazing process I never could've imagined.

I'd been especially willing to try to dupe the range-finding committee for that taste bud question because I really did think the item and rubric worked. The question asked the student for four very specific things (favorite food, its flavor, where that was found on the tongue, and how taste worked), and the rubric subsequently allocated points based on the presence of those four things. As far as I was concerned, that was a very reasonable way to dole out points, as I'd seen other situations where the connection between item and rubric was not so strong: I'd seen items ask for something (like a student's favorite food or where tastes are found on the tongue) but then have the rubric give no credit for providing those answers, and I'd seen questions asking the student for maybe two things but the rubric expecting them to find three. On my taste bud question, however, the students earned points based very simply on whether they did what the item asked. That I approved of.

I expected it wouldn't be hard to score the item. I imagined a simple process where we would credit the students' favorite foods, the subsequent flavors of those foods (candy was sweet, popcorn was salty, lemon was sour, etc.), the correct placements of those tastes on the tongue (sweet and salty on the front of the tongue, sour on the side, and bitter in the back), and the identification of the "taste buds" or "papillae" as vital to the tasting process. I figured if I got some reasonably intelligent scorers to train, we would waltz through the scoring of that item without even slowing down.

Ha!

While Harlan and Maria (she was training the writing scoring) were working the day shift in Tucson, I was on the night shift, me and 48 scorers working from 6 P.M. to 10:30 P.M. every evening. The scorers were a perfectly sensible bunch, some retirees and some ex-military, but mostly people taking on second jobs in the evenings after eight hours of work each day.

Although it was the first time I'd taught a group to score, not to mention the first time I'd been in charge of 50-odd people, the training went well. People agreed with the Anchor Papers and correctly scored the Practice Papers. There was some debate about some papers, of course, but not enough that caused any real consternation. I thought I handed it all deftly, providing what I figured were both helpful clarifications and occasional witty asides. In no time my group was pretty much in accord, and by the end of the training, I imagined they were my happy minions and I was their beloved leader.

Surveying my kingdom from my perch at the head table, I watched as the group started to score, and I was amused to see them reading responses and counting on their hands. One, two, three, four, they were counting, fingers in the air, before penciling in what I hoped were the correct answers on their score sheets.

My scorers were a fine bunch of people, and they went out of their way to make me feel at home. They gave me suggestions for the weekends, telling me what I should see (the Arizona–Sonora Desert Museum) and do (drive up Mount Lemon) and giving me recommendations on where to find the best steak or the best margarita in town. One night one of the scorers provided me a home-cooked dinner (lasagna, garlic bread, a salad), and a couple of others flirted with me regularly, insisting I needed to accompany them to the Hotel Congress for drinks or Café Poca Cosa for dinner.

In return for my scorers' generosity of spirit and general goodwill, and because by 10:00 P.M. every night I needed a cocktail, most nights we cut out a little early. Sometimes I told them to wrap it up at 10:25, sometimes at 10:15, although one night at 10 o'clock I took a quick survey of the group and made a well-received management decision.

"OK, folks," I asked. "Who's bored out of their skulls?"

Every single person's hand shot skyward, and getting 100 percent agreement from the crowd—the sort of consensus we normally only dreamed of in the world of standardized testing—I decided to call it a night.

"Thought so," I told them. "Go ahead and put down on your timesheets that you worked 'til 10:30, but head on home right now."

The cheers for me rang throughout the room. I was adored!

And it was a good thing I was so revered, too, because the *scoring* of the project went to hell that very first night. During the first hour I'd seen a scorer occasionally ask a table leader a question, but mostly the process seemed to be going smoothly. Then one of the table leaders came up to address me, at which point my education in assessment really began.

Layla was a fourth-grade teacher during the day, and though we were working on a fourth-grade item, she was confused. "Todd," she asked, "exactly what is the correct flavor for pizza?"

I didn't even have to think about it. "'Delicious,'" I smiled.

"Yes," she said, not particularly amused, "but all these kids are claiming pizza is their favorite food and then saying it's sweet, it's salty, it's bitter."

"Oh."

"So what's the correct answer?"

Her name was Layla, but thereafter I considered her Pandora. I knew very well the trouble that would ensue.

"What do you think?" I asked.

She shrugged. "Salty, for sure, but maybe sweet, too. The tomato sauce . . . ."

Ken, another table leader, had come up to join the discussion. "The correct flavor of pizza?" he asked. "That's what I came up to ask, too."

"And?"

"Certainly salty, yes. And sweet. But I could see sour or bitter."

"Bitter pizza?" I scoffed. "I don't think so." This was the very sort of discussion I'd seen at every scoring session, but because I imagined I was a particularly enlightened trainer, I thought I'd hammer this little fiasco out immediately. I sent Layla and Ken back to their tables and addressed the crowd.

"Excuse me, folks," I said, "let's take a moment to clear something up."

My scorers took their fingers out of the air, laid their pencils down, and gave me their undivided opinions. "Pizza," I asked, "what are you crediting as the correct flavor?"

No one offered any immediate answers.

"There are no wrong answers," I said. "We just need to come to some consensus."

"I've been crediting salty," a woman said. People nodded in agreement.

"I've been crediting sweet," a man replied. "The pineapple, I thought." More nodding from around the room.

"I took sour once," a guy offered. Mostly people shook their heads no, but a couple shrugged "maybe."

"Sour?" I asked, rolling my eyes. "How do you figure?"

"Anchovies?" he said. "Some people get artichokes or feta cheese."

"Artichokes are bitter."

"Or peppers," someone added. "Are they sour? Bitter?"

"Onions?"

"What about jalapeños?" The group that had been so quiet a second ago now wouldn't shut up.

"Hold on," I said, deciding to make my decree. "So certainly we have to credit both salty and sweet as the correct taste for pizza. And I guess . . . ."

The entire group awaited my proclamation.

"I guess we have to credit sour, too." I hoped that would put an end to it.

A guy at the table closest to me spoke. He looked like a troublemaker to me, the intransigent type who might dare to doubt me. "What about bitter?" he asked.

"I don't think so," I said omnisciently, shaking my head. "I can't see how pizza can be bitter." I figured my wise decision would end all debate.

"Anchovies, if you don't like 'em," a woman said.

"Jalapeños, if they're not your thing," someone answered.

"Everyone's taste is different," the wise guy from the near table said. "Who knows what different people think is bitter?"

His argument had gained momentum, and people from around the room were beginning to agree. They were getting standardized *without* me. My eyes narrowed as I looked at this guy, leading a little coup, he was.

"OK," I said. "Is that what you all think? Can pizza be *any* taste, then? Hands in the air." And sure enough, almost everyone raised their hands, the bunch of them wanting to credit the correct flavor of pizza as salty *or* sweet *or* sour *or* bitter.

"You're saying anything goes?" I asked them, and they shrugged and nodded. Given they mostly all agreed, and given the correct answer for the taste of pizza had never been predetermined, we took all *four* of the options listed in the article as the correct answer for the flavor of pizza.

"All right," I said, heading back to my own desk. "Good luck and back to it."

"What about ice cream?" a woman yelled.

I stopped in my tracks. "Ice cream?" I asked, barely daring to turn around.

"What's its correct flavor?"

"C'mon," I said. "Ice cream? I worked in an ice cream factory during college, so this is my area of expertise."

"And?"

"Ice cream is *sweet*!" I smiled. "I used to eat about a gallon of it a day, sticking my hand into every flavor that came off the assembly line. Definitely sweet."

"I agree," the woman said. "But I had a kid say his favorite food was pistachio ice cream, and he said it was salty."

I frowned. Damn those kids! Since I didn't see how you couldn't credit that, salty was added to the list of acceptable responses for the flavor of ice cream.

"What about sour?" someone asked.

"No," I said. "Ice cream is *not* sour." At sour I would draw the line.

"Lemon sherbet."

And so it was that the correct flavor for ice cream, as it had been for pizza, was finally identified as sweet *or* sour *or* salty *or* bitter. In no time, after a brief discussion about candy (dark chocolate? milk chocolate? milk chocolate with *peanuts*? *sour* balls? *saltwater* taffy? Mary-Janes?), *and* popcorn (popcorn with *butter*? *caramel* popcorn? popcorn with cayenne *pepper*? with celery *salt*?), *and* vegetables (squash? squash with *butter*? with *brown sugar*? with *salt and pepper*? cucumbers with *vinegar*? potatoes with *sour cream*?), it was decided the correct flavor for any of the student's favorite foods would be sweet *or* sour *or* salty *or* bitter.

If a kid said his favorite food was ice cream and he said it was bitter, we credited both answers. If he said his favorite food was spinach and it was sweet, ditto. *Any* of the four options listed in the article would be credited as the flavor of *any* favorite food. What else was there to do? Who were we to tell some kid what his favorite food tasted like? Maybe that's not what a teacher from that state would have done, but it was 10 o'clock at night in the Arizona desert and those teachers were probably asleep, 1,700 miles away. The decisions fell to me, so I made them.

After the Great Taste Debate, that first night went without incident, but by the time we'd readjourned the next evening, the questions began anew. Layla was back to bother me again, this time joined not by Ken but by a third table leader, Linda. The two of them wanted to know my stance on a student's favorite food: could a student really say *anything* was his or her favorite food? They understood the question was asking for a personal opinion, but was *anything* acceptable? As I heard their arguments, I thought the two of them were being annoying—couldn't they use a little common sense? Their complaints seemed a little dramatic, and I couldn't imagine my well-trained scorers were having any difficulty with the "favorite food" part of the rubric. I decided to take the argument straight to my people.

"Good evening, folks," I said them, "Welcome to Night 2." They smiled at me, quite fondly, I still thought.

"Let's talk about acceptable answers for the students' favorite foods," I said. "Obviously, this part of the item is asking for the student's personal opinion about what they like to eat, so in theory *anything* should be accepted."

My people looked at me, not saying a word. I *knew* they were with me, I thought. "You guys having any problem with that?" I said.

They didn't seem to be. Even the smug little bastard at the nearest table agreed, although when he started talking I ended up hating him more. "Obviously we've got to accept whatever a kid says," the guy offered.

I nodded my head in agreement, looking around the room, making eye contact with the scorers and tacitly asking them, "Right?"

But the know-it-all continued. "That's why I've had to accept 'dirt' a couple of times."

My head jerked in his direction. "What?" I asked him. "Are you serious?"

He was unfazed. "Of course," he said. "You said during training that *any* answer was acceptable."

"But dirt? Are you out of your mind?"

People laughed. Layla and Linda, at the end of their respective tables, shook their heads knowingly. Both of their faces said "I told you so."

"Dirt?!" It was my turn to be incredulous. "Is anyone else accepting 'dirt'?" I spit the word out.

"I accepted it, too, because you said—," someone started.

"I didn't credit it," another answered.

"I asked Layla, and she said maybe."

I interrupted them. I felt like it was the NAEP range-finding committee all over again, when it was time for me to be the voice of reason.

"Let's not be ridiculous here. I don't need any other opinions on this, and I'm telling you right now that dirt is *not* acceptable as a favorite food. Never," I shook my head in disgust. "How 'bout a little common sense, people?"

No one said anything, and some of them looked a little wounded. I knew very well they were thinking, "But you said . . . ."

"What about grass?" a guy asked.

"Grass?" I repeated.

"Yeah, I've got that a couple of times."

"And what did you do with it?" I questioned.

"I credited it."

"You *credited* it?"

"Me, too," came another reply. "You said anything counted."

"Not anything you put in your mouth, people!" I said. "Your favorite *food*!" I was amazed.

"Who here would accept grass as a favorite food?" I asked the group.

There was very little response to my question. "Hands in the air," I said. "Who would accept grass?"

Maybe a third of the hands in the room were raised, and maybe a third of the hands in the room stayed down. The rest of the scorers seemed to abstain. I smiled a bitter smile.

"Fine," I said, realizing Layla and Linda had been right. Even the students' favorite foods was an issue, so I began to address it. I asked my scorers about any dubious answers they'd seen, and we had a lengthy discussion about them, eventually writing down (on a whiteboard beside my desk) as comprehensive a list as possible of all the acceptable and unacceptable responses:

FAVORITE FOODS

Acceptable Responses

Food (of any kind)	Candy
Beef Jerky	Sugar
Water	Salt
Soda	Pepper
Gum	Ice Cubes
Big League Chew	Pine Sap (Gum)

Unacceptable Responses

Toothpaste	Sticks
Toothpicks	Pine Needles
Styrofoam	Chewing Tobacco
Plastic Straws	Beer/Wine/Liquor
Rocks	Cat Food
Dirt	Dog Food
Mud	Bait
Grass	Worms
Twigs	Night Crawlers
Leaves	"My thumb"

It all engendered considerable debate, much more than I would have anticipated. At some point I was trying to make hard and fast rules that would eliminate the absurd answers like "dirt" even being considered, but that never worked. When I tried to establish a rule that a favorite food had to have "nutritional value" to be credited, that meant dirt was out but grass was in. When I tried to establish it was simply a matter of "calories," suddenly water couldn't be credited when I always thought it should. When finally I settled on the idea of a favorite food needing to provide "sustenance," a number of people pointed out that beer, wine, and liquor could definitely do that.

"You're telling me," I muttered.

For a week we scored that item, and having conceded any flavor/taste was acceptable with any favorite food, I still had to lead discussions about foods we could accept (ice cubes) and foods we could not (glass, tree bark, pencil erasers). At some point I was explaining we could not accept mud as a favorite food, because while mud's components consisted of one acceptable response (water), it also consisted of one unacceptable response (dirt), meaning ultimately that answer had to be tossed on the "no" pile.

It was the same with the placement of tastes. While our rubric clearly delineated what the acceptable responses were (sweet and salty on the front of tongue, sour on the side, and bitter in the back), there were still questions: What if sweet was listed as being on the front *and* back of the tongue, which was half right and half wrong? What if a student said he tasted strawberries "everywhere" on the tongue, which was somewhat true and mostly not? What if he said the "bitter" taste of nails was experienced at the back of the tongue, which was correct expect for that bothersome little fact that nails shouldn't be tasted? What if he said "ice cream" was "bitter," which we would *generously* accept, but then said "bitter" was found in the "front" of the tongue, which although wrong really was the place a student would experience the taste of ice cream? What to do then?

Every time I tried to have a group discussion to clear up some little issue, more little issues would come to light. At the end of most of these confabs, my scorers looked more confused than before I'd begun, and I'd be weaving about punch-drunk, staggered by their questions like a boxer who'd been socked in the jaw.

"What *about* sweet potatoes?" I asked the scorer who brought them up.

"Are sweet potatoes worth one point or two?" he said.

"Huh?" I eloquently replied.

"Is sweet potatoes both a favorite food and a taste or just a favorite food?"

"What are you talking about?"

"I think sweet potatoes should get two points, for identifying the favorite food of potatoes and the taste of sweet, but Layla said no."

I thought the guy was insane. "And why did you say no, Layla?" I asked her.

"Because I think that's idiotic," she answered. "The student has clearly given us their favorite food, and it happens to include the word *sweet* in it. The response otherwise never IDs a flavor for sweet potatoes."

"Well done," I told her.

"I was trying to help the kid out," the errant scorer said.

"That's not your job," I told him. "Credit what's on the page, not what you can make work through whatever generous machinations are going on in your head."

"I thought we were supposed to find the most points there were?" the guy said.

From around the room a couple of "yeahs" and "me, toos" were heard.

"You're not supposed to *find* anything," I said. "It's not a bloody scavenger hunt! You should be crediting what the student *purposefully* did."

Some people grimaced at that; some nodded; some pursed their lips. One guy raised his hand to argue, but I ignored him, opting instead to tell my group to keep scoring as I headed back to the refuge of my desk. The last bit on the rubric (that taste was experienced on the "taste buds" or the "papillae") went largely unquestioned, but that was the only easy thing about the whole item. It all otherwise seemed a mess, and by the time we were done scoring that question, I was seriously at odds with what I thought was an entire room full of nattering dimwits—they were nice people, but . . . .

As the scoring progressed, I became more and more on edge. When anyone approached to ask a question, I may have looked calm, but inside I was a nervous wreck. While on my face I kept a mask of utter equanimity, in my head I was twitching uncontrollably, rocking back and forth like Rain Man, chanting to myself, "I am an excellent scorer, an excellent scorer . . . ."

One thing about the whole ordeal was pretty ironic, though. I realized, in my suffering, that Harlan and I had been right in keeping those teachers at the range-finding committee in the dark regarding the reality of standardized test scoring: what they didn't know *couldn't* hurt them.

At that point, the reality of standardized test scoring could hurt only me.

After successfully completing that reading project, I flew east to another of NCS's scoring sites. Leaving the sunny desert behind, I got to East Lansing on a wet Sunday night, only to wake up the next morning to find myself in a hellhole in Michigan. Instead of the great hotel suite I'd had in Arizona (four rooms, two balconies, views of the Catalina Mountains from every window), I was plopped down in a moldy motel, across a pot-holed parking lot from the East Lansing scoring center. In that building, Maria and I found a musty room with no windows filled with insolent scorers, the bunch of them none too thrilled we were replacing Annie, the beloved trainer who'd been shipped back to Iowa City. Wildly unpopular with those East Lansing folks, Maria and I still soldiered on with the training, fighting against both the disdain of those scorers *and* the massive roars of the huge trains that sped by our windows every hour, on the hour.

If those scorers wanted their last trainer back, Maria and I wanted our last scorers back. We missed sunny Tucson. The only thing that made the work palatable for me was the fact we were training an eastern state's "Standards of Learning" writing assessment, a test that state shortened to call the "SOLs." Whenever I thought I was too depressed to continue working in that building I just thought of the SOLs, if only because that acronym had always meant "shit outta luck" to me. I was tickled every time I thought it.

What wasn't funny about the SOLs was not only was it essay scoring, but it was *three-trait* essay scoring. Instead of giving a single score to each essay, our employees would give *three* scores to each: a score for composition, a score for written expression, and a score for grammar. To begin with, Maria and I didn't *exactly* get the difference between the "composition" score and the "written expression" score, and when we asked the state Department of Education representative for clarification, she basically demurred—she may have talked eloquently in her honeyed, southern accent, but what she said didn't amount to much.

That wasn't the only confusion. We heard the usual bit about murky rubric language, and Maria or I would be in front of that unhappy crowd trying to explain why some essay was a 4, said to "demonstrate consistent, although not necessarily perfect, control of almost all of the domain's features," when some scorer was arguing it was a 3, demonstrating only "reasonable, but not consistent, control of most of the domain's features." Plus, the three scores weren't helping much, either: when previously we'd had to lead lengthy discussions about whether an essay deserved a 3 or a 4, now Maria and I were in charge of debates about whether an essay deserved a 343 or a 432, the expansion of the rubric from one to three scores really no more than a chance for disagreements to expand exponentially.

Somehow those scorers in Michigan all passed the qualifying tests—Maria and I were more than a little convinced the omnipotent erasers may have played a part—and we were fortunately able to escape East Lansing for good. Maria headed home to Iowa, while I flew back to Tucson, where I would train and supervise another writing assessment. Although it was great to be back in the desert, the less said about that final assessment, the better. It was a third-grade writing test, although the rubric being used was the vaunted 6 × 6 scoring guide, meaning each essay written by those eight-year-olds would get six scores (*six*, I say), from the low of 1 to the high of 6 for six different domains: ideas, organization, voice, word choice, sentence fluency, and conventions.

The idea any group could *consistently* score those essays using that rubric could only be called optimistic. I'm not saying the rubric didn't work, just that it's impossible to imagine you can expect grown-ups to agree *six different times* when assessing those brief student responses. The rubric was considerably longer than the essays themselves, and elementary school students aren't all a bunch of budding Shakespeares, either. Mostly those kids were just spouting off, writing whatever popped into their heads.

I would be standing in front of a crowd of earnest test scorers, all of us staring down at the same student response:

Grade 3
Descriptive Prompt

Write about your favorite day. It can be a day that happened only once or may have happened many times. Be specific in explaining your good day.

Friday was a good day. Its pizza day at school. I luve pizzae. The best part about it is the cheez. Plus its one of the three dayz we get resess. Resess is my best part of school so   my best day has to be on a day when we do have. Mrs Wyndum let's us play what games we want at resass so that is fun. Jungle jim, jamborre, kickball whatever we want. Other recess days are not fun because we have to do grup things. Walking running togethr is not as cool as playing whatever u want. The day I do not like is monday. On monday we have no resess and lunch, is raveole. I hate that food. The stuff in it is gros. Mondays are the worse. Friday is the best.

"So," I might ask, "what do we think of this essay's ideas? On a scale of 1 to 6, are they 'excellent' ideas or 'adequate ideas'?"

The scorers looked at me like I was mad. They glanced down at the slew of simple sentences in front of them and back up at me. "Not sure," one might say. "Is the idea of pizza insightful for an eight-year-old, or is it pedestrian?"

"I'd say it's quite deep for a third grader," another might joke. "Plus, wham, out of the blue, this inspired concept of 'recess.' Wow, I didn't see that coming!"

"People," I would warn. "Focus!" Still, they couldn't help themselves and soon enough would be giggling in response to the exhaustive discussions I was trying to lead about these short, little essays scribbled by short, little tots.

"How about the student's writing style?" I would ask. "How is the voice? The word choice? The sentence fluency?"

"Great word choice," someone would say. "The kid said 'recess' and then repeated it 18 times."

"Not sure about that," another might add, "but there is some nice sentence variety here. A lot of the sentences have four words, but some even have *five*."

Eventually I gave up. Instead of attempting to discuss the relative literary merits of each third grader's response, I'd just tell the scorers how the state committee had assessed each essay.

"The official score for this paper is 445434," I might say.

"No way!" someone would argue. "I gave it a 555343."

"A 555343? That's absurd. It's clearly a 456445."

"A 456445? Are you drunk?! This is a . . . ."

As much as I tried not to, sometimes I just had to laugh. Imagine, the work we were doing was supposedly part of the "standardized" testing industry.

A Real Job

AFTER GETTING rejected by the Writer's Workshop, I had no better plan than to slog away in testing. I may not have wanted to, but I faced a number of obstacles in advancing into any other line of work. First, I was living in a place where the percentages were against me, because Iowa City was a burg full of well-educated townies and very few jobs. Second, my grandiose sense of self continued to flourish unabated, and because I still imagined myself a writer and possible genius, I wasn't ecstatic about the idea of some career in Iowa City at a shipping company, meat-packing plant, or the university's administrative offices.

Instead, I went on the dole. After completing a four-month project for Maria in January 1999, I stopped working. There were no scoring projects happening and hence nothing for me to do. Per Greg's suggestion, I dropped in to the state unemployment office, where I happily discovered I could get checks every week for not doing anything. While I'd always been fundamentally opposed to receiving such government largesse, I was even more opposed to demeaning myself by actually, you know, looking for work. The clerk at the unemployment office took down my vital information and, after hearing I'd been working at NCS for years, told me I didn't even have to apply for other jobs to get my government payouts. Because the state could reasonably expect I would work again at NCS every couple of months, they were willing to pay me to remain unemployed.

After hearing that promising news, I meandered downtown to enjoy a crossword puzzle and a patty melt at the Hamburg Inn, and for the next couple of months I did nothing but receive checks. I did feel a little bad about it, because I was a perfectly healthy and capable guy who could certainly get *some* job. Getting paid *not* to work didn't seem quite right. But I cashed the checks, and I used the money to maintain my life of soccer playing, book reading, and recreational drinking.

By March, however, NCS was again offering me work. While I didn't love the idea of scoring more tests, I agreed because the company wanted me to lead projects in Minnesota and Michigan, an offer I couldn't refuse. I dug the travel and life on an expense account too much. I spent four weeks in Minneapolis that spring managing the scoring of a reading test, a trip most notable for my many visits to Murray's Steakhouse (try the sumptuous "silver butter-knife" New York strip steak, but only if you're not paying) and the fact a number of the supervisors on the project had been offered jobs only after successfully completing rehab. Although NCS might not have wanted to emphasize that fact, I thought it would've been a great idea to publicize that not only were every one of NCS's temporary employees graduates of a *college*, some were also graduates of one of the finest drug and alcohol treatment programs in all the land.

The four weeks after Minnesota I spent in East Lansing, managing the scoring of another reading test, and while that town didn't offer the dining options of Minneapolis and that project didn't have such an interesting staff, I did have one memorable experience there. Returning from a trip for coffee one day, I was informed by the site manager (himself a temporary employee) that in my absence an angry husband had busted into the site and tried to drag out his estranged wife. As my mouth dropped open, a rush of horror flashing through me, the site manager smiled and calmed me, saying everything was under control.

"Don't worry about it," he said, "I called the cops and got my pistol from the car."

At the end of that project I was happy to escape East Lansing and return to Iowa, even if that meant no more paychecks and no more expense account. Still, it was good to get back to Iowa City for the summer, back to my life of unemployment and unemployment checks. Months slipped lazily and happily by, although at some point I did begin to think maybe I needed more. By then I was 33 years old—the age Jesus was when he died—and if I looked at things objectively, I had to concede he'd probably made more of his life.

Recognizing it was time for a change, I decided to take a big step: I would go to Africa to visit my brother Cary. Cary lived in Tanzania and had often invited me over, but I'd been either too busy or too scared to bother. Having a little midlife crisis, though, I thought Africa sounded like an excellent idea, so in January 2000, I jetted off to Nairobi. For six weeks I traveled through East Africa, on safari in Kenya and Tanzania and fishing off the island of Lamu. My African adventure included the normal majestic scenery and exotic animals, but I also found myself the target of attacking bull elephants, lurking schools of sharks, and a number of scheming pickpockets and con men. Because a wave of robberies was sweeping its way through Cary's neighborhood in Tanzania, I spent my last two evenings under virtual house arrest, my brother and I barricaded inside his home inside a walled compound, his three armed guards and seven dogs patrolling the grounds outside.

Lying in bed and listening to the sounds of the chattering machine guns echoing through the night, Cary and I waited nervously for what seemed an inevitable assault.

Fortunately, it didn't happen, and I was happy to return home to Iowa City. While my trip had been thrilling, it hadn't exactly changed me, and in no time I was back at NCS working on the 2000 NAEP science test. I was hired to be a "scoring supervisor," which basically meant I was the first level of management overseeing a group of 10 scorers. At one time that job had been called "table leader," but NCS had fully committed itself to corporate-speak and decided it would add a little gravitas to the position by increasing the number of syllables in its title.

I had been a *scorer* on the 1996 NAEP science test. I distinctly recall working at the NCS site on Boyrum Street, leaning back in my chair with my feet on the desk as I stared at the computer screen, scanning and skimming my way through thousands and thousands of student responses. I held a notebook in my lap and the computer mouse atop that, clicking away for days as we scored items about soil erosion, planetary rotation, and the functioning of pendulums. I had very little experience in the world of science—few of us NCS scorers did—but the ETS trainers filled our heads with just enough information we could search out key words and ideas and then slap down some (hopefully appropriate) score.

Most memorable about 1996 NAEP science was the woman in charge of the project for ETS. Olivia was her name, a short, little Brit who spoke in a clipped, English accent and dressed each day from head to toe in black. Olivia was the Tasmanian Devil of standardized testing that year, easily overseeing the scoring of dozens of science items and hundreds of thousands of student responses as she raced from cubicle to cubicle to answer questions, solve problems, and end debates. Olivia seemed to have in her head both an encyclopedic knowledge of all things science *and* the entire catalog of NAEP rubrics our groups were using to score, and we knew when Olivia made a decision, it stood. She may have had a sly sense of humor and a dry, British wit, but we also knew what Olivia said went, no questions asked. Given my experience in '96, I was happy to see Olivia remained in charge of the NAEP science project for ETS in 2000. I was also happy (although not at first) that she seemed to know who I was.

"Yes, Todd," she said. "You used to sit there with your feet on the desk."

"Uh . . . ," I stammered.

"Don't worry about it," she laughed. "As long as you kept scoring."

When one of her staff wasn't able to come from Princeton to train 2000 NAEP science, Olivia promoted me, so instead of being a "scoring supervisor" for the project I ended up a "trainer." *After* she gave me the job, Olivia asked me about my experience.

"What do you know about science?" she quizzed me.

"Well . . ." I said, trying to think something up.

"You'll figure it out," she said.

I nodded my thanks, vowing to get directly to the Internet to learn all I could about the natural world.

Training NAEP science didn't end up being much different than training any other project (i.e., I trained, the scorers argued or were confused or disagreed, and ultimately the scoring supervisor worked some statistical tomfoolery on his or her computer to make it all look good), except for one large difference: Trend. NAEP is called the "National Assessment for Educational *Progress*" because *identical* NAEP tests are given every four years (or every two years, nowadays), meaning the tests are believed to show the progress—or lack thereof— occurring within U.S. schools for certain subject areas. To be statistically valid, the NAEP tests need to be scored the same way every time they are administered, so NCS scorers have to pass "Trend Tests" every day to show they are scoring responses the same way they were scored in previous years. That meant those of us in the cubicles in Iowa City scoring the 2000 NAEP science test had to both earn acceptable reliabilities within our group (agreement between our 10 scorers) *and* pass a Trend Test (getting an acceptable agreement between our group and the 1996 group when scoring a sample of 1996 responses).

Getting those acceptable numbers was the hardest thing about 2000 NAEP science, because failing to pass a Trend Test meant a group would have to retrain, and that was a fate no one relished—retraining meant more work and a whole lot of arguing. Worse, it was especially hard to get good numbers in 2000 because the new, computer-based scoring system was harder to manipulate than the old one had been. When in 1994 Greg first told me he could "make statistics dance," that was because he could improve reliability numbers simply by changing scores in the system that didn't agree. By 2000, the system had been "improved" so when a supervisor changed a wrong score to match a correct one, the reliability number *didn't* go up. That way, it was said, the reliability statistics would more accurately reflect the real agreement percentages between scorers.

In theory, that should have been true. The problem, however, was that thesis failed to consider the ingenious ways my supervisor friends and I continued to find to doctor the statistics. Necessity is the mother of invention, and all of us temporary NCS supervisors—hourly workers with nothing on the line and deadlines to meet—found newer and better ways to beat the system. My friend Scott took the easiest route, explaining his method one day at break.

"Do you have a scorer or two who doesn't know what he's doing?" he asked.

Everyone nodded. "Of course," people laughed.

"That would be Butch on my team," Scott said. "So when we're scoring papers for this year's project, I set Butch up on his computer so he's actually scoring a bunch of 1996 papers that don't matter. That way, he doesn't screw with our reliability."

The listening crowd approved. "Very nice."

"And when we have to pass Trend," Scott continued, "I set Butch up to score year 2000 papers, so he has no effect. It's like he's not even in the system for Trend."

"Brilliant," we laughed. While maybe it would have been easier for Scott to get Butch taken off the project, that meant Scott—a temporary employee—would be costing Butch—another temporary employee—his job. No one had the heart for that, so everyone fudged the statistics instead.

The easiest way to control the reliability was to be aware of second-scoring. Because only 25 percent of NAEP papers were scored two times, those were the only responses that counted toward reliability. As long as the scorers managed to score those student responses within the acceptable reliability range, the remaining three-quarters of the student responses really didn't matter. Fortunately, it was possible for the scorers to see on their computers (from a bar in the bottom right corner of the screen) when they were second-scoring, and most made a point to share those answers with the rest of the group to ensure matching scores would be given.

"Who scored this?" someone might ask. "It says 'because Earth rotates on its axis.'"

"I had that," another would answer. "I gave that a 3."

"A 3?"

"Yup."

"OK. A 3 it is."

"What about 'because it spins'?" another would ask.

"I gave that a 2."

Conversations like that were heard constantly, in every cubicle, simple discussions that helped foster acceptable numbers. The questions were never about what a student response might have *deserved*; the questions were only about what score to give to ensure statistical agreement.

The entire industry's obsession with statistics was something I never understood, as most scoring projects seemed more fixated on getting good numbers on the myriad reports that existed (group reliability reports, individual reliability reports, score distribution reports, rate reports, etc.) than in getting correct scores put on to student responses. That illogical obsession became abundantly clear to me on my last day scoring 2000 NAEP science, when on the Saturday after the project ended, Brian, the NCS scoring director, called me in to the office to help Olivia finish up the few remaining items.

"OK," Olivia told me, "you and I have to score one last question in its entirety because it was lost in the system. Now we found it and have to score all 1,200 student responses by ourselves."

"Let's do it," I said, Olivia and I settling in front of a couple of computers. Olivia handed me an illustration of a marine food chain and a scoring rubric, explaining how both worked.

"Three-point item," she said. "Three points for identifying two predators in the food chain, two points for identifying one predator, and one point for identifying no predators. Got it?"

I scanned the picture of the food chain in front of me. I looked at the rubric. "Got it," I said.

So we began to score student responses, Olivia and I, the two of us sitting in an otherwise empty NCS scoring center. Occasionally I would ask her a question ("Is 'shrimp' acceptable? Do they prey on anything?"), and occasionally she would offer me some advice ("This is the first time I've seen this, but don't forget to credit 'tuna'"), but mostly we sat quietly and scored, click, click, click. Given Olivia was an expert in science and the person most responsible for the development of that item and rubric, *and* given I was smart enough to figure out that simple scoring guide and ask Olivia if I had any questions, I began to have an unusual feeling about the job she and I were doing. As we clicked away, I had the altogether strange sensation maybe standardized test scoring *could* work.

Instead of the bedlam that usually occurred when you had 10 or 20 temporary employees trying to agree as they scored innumerable student responses in a subject area they may or may not have understood, it seemed Olivia and I were giving out 3's to the student responses that deserved 3's, 2's to the responses that deserved 2's, and 1's to the responses that deserved 1's. Along with giving the correct scores, she and I were also working cohesively, agreeing with each other—we were actually scoring in a *standardized* way. For one of the first times in my test-scoring experience, I was completely confident about the work being done.

"Of course," Olivia said, interrupting my reverie, "you do realize this is completely illegitimate, right? We're not allowed to have only two people score an entire item."

"Why not? This is the first time I've thought the process was working."

"The psychometricians say no," she said. "'Not a valid sample,' they say."

"But we're putting the correct scores on the student responses!"

"Not the issue," she said. "Check our reliability."

Clicking through the reports, I found the number showing the agreement between my scores and Olivia's. "Look!" I said. "We have 96 percent agreement! Test scoring *can* be done in a standardized way."

Olivia grimaced. "Now check the 1996 reliability for the item."

Again I scrolled through the computer's reports, until I found the agreement numbers for that previous group. "Eighty-five percent," I said. "Not bad."

"Bad for us," Olivia replied. "Our reliability is 11 points higher than theirs. We have to be within seven points of their reliability, or the item gets thrown out."

"Thrown out?"

"Never used again. It's considered statistically invalid if the reliability numbers are seven points higher or seven points lower than the previous year's."

I considered that for a second. "So you and I are agreeing with each other *too often?*"

"We are doing *too well*," Olivia smiled bitterly. "Now go get Brian to join us, so we can disagree a little more frequently."

That's exactly what happened. Olivia set Brian up to score the item, too, and while Brian was a perfectly intelligent fellow, Olivia didn't give him a lot of advice, so by the time we'd finished scoring, our group reliability had dropped from 96 to 91 percent.

Just in time! At 91 percent reliability, we were finally disagreeing with each other enough that we were within seven points of the 1996 statistics. At last our work was legitimate, because with the addition of Brian, we had *three* scorers working on the item, and we had attained acceptable numbers. Sure, at 91 percent, Brian, Olivia, and I may have been scoring in a less standardized manner than just Olivia and I had, but at least adding Brian to the mix had saved the day: enough *disagreements* had gotten into the reliability pool that the item could be saved.

Whew! That was close! We had failed just enough that the item could succeed.

When the NAEP science project ended, I went quickly back on the dole, but shortly thereafter Maria hooked me up with a consulting job. She told me AIR (American Institutes of Research, a research company located in our nation's capital) needed personnel to train the scoring of the essay portion of the California High School Exit Exam (CAHSEE). CAHSEE was one of the first exit exams in the country, in its pilot stages, but in upcoming years that mandatory test would be one every high school student in California would have to pass to earn their diploma. Welcoming both the chance to be involved with that groundbreaking test and the big money AIR was paying ($25 an hour!), I agreed to the job. I thought there would probably be some travel in it for me, too. Los Angeles or Washington, DC, I figured, here I come!

Not exactly. While AIR did hire me to train scorers for the essay portion of CAHSEE, my travels for that job took me no farther than Iowa City. In fact, my commute took me only three miles up the road from my Brown Street home, right back to the NCS scoring center where I had just worked on NAEP science. While I was annoyed I didn't get to make any exciting business trips on the AIR dime, I had another thought, too: did NCS score *every* test in the country? Given I'd scored national, state, and local tests for NCS at its scoring centers all across America, it was beginning to seem the company had a complete monopoly on the entire test-scoring business.

Regardless, as an AIR consultant, I returned to the NCS scoring center in Iowa City to train their scorers on assessing essays for CAHSEE. Although CAHSEE had different prompts than I'd ever seen before and a different rubric (not better, not worse, just different), much about the scoring project remained unchanged: the same trainer trained (me), the same supervisors supervised, and the same scorers scored. It was business as usual, in every way. Without getting into the specifics of it, I'd say the scoring of the CAHSEE essays was exactly as efficacious as the scoring of any other project I'd ever been associated with.

Uh-huh. It was *exactly* as efficacious.

The good news was that then I had contacts at AIR, and those contacts were pleased with my work. When the CAHSEE essay scoring was done, AIR offered me a consulting job writing test questions and test passages for them, which is how I spent the summer of 2000. Lazing about my apartment, scratching the ears of my cats and joining them for frequent naps, I wrote numerous multiple-choice questions and short stories for the CAHSEE test. The questions paid $25 a pop, and the stories paid $500, and in one burst of creativity alone I wrote six stories about my trip to Africa, racking up three grand in less than a week—basically I paid for my six weeks on the Dark Continent in those six, short days' work. It was easy money, and the cats and I were convinced I'd found my destiny: lollygagging about my apartment and writing for money were exactly what I wanted to do.

The other benefit of my work at AIR was it helped flesh out my résumé. At NCS I'd spent years scoring tests and writing rubrics, and I'd also gained a wealth of experience supervising people, training groups, and even running professional development seminars for teachers. My AIR work had included test *development* (writing questions and stories), and between those two companies I had what looked on paper like an actual career in standardized testing. By then it was the summer of 2000, and I'd reached a point I thought it might be nice to have health insurance. I decided, therefore, I wanted a "real job," and I quickly parlayed my shiny new résumé and industry connections into a full-time gig at Educational Testing Service, the mother ship of the assessment world.

In October 2000, I moved to Princeton to work for ETS, on its sylvan campus of rolling hills and wandering geese. I was given a huge office with two desks and a view of the forest outside, and for 37.5 hours a week, I was expected to sit in my plush chair, fooling around on the computer, a cog in the machine of the great standardized testing industry. While I did work, I can't say I worked very hard—I ended up with exactly no sweat on my brow or calluses on my fingers.

My boss was none other than the "Princeton matron," Clarice. She was a spitfire, a tiny woman of Italian descent who'd earned a PhD to escape life in the Midwest and was now living on the East Coast, She'd used her degrees and teaching experience to make a career in "education." I loved working for Clarice, because she was cynical, funny, and oh-so-smart, and the two of us had exactly the same commitment to corporate culture. Most mornings Clarice would waltz into my office at about 10 o'clock and ask what I was up to.

"Let's see," I'd say, pretending to hide the SportsIllustrated.com Web site on my computer screen, "I'm . . . uh . . . 'writing a report on bias and sensitivity'?" I'd make air quotes around the imaginary job.

"Feckless," Clarice would mutter, "absolutely feckless."

As she walked out of my office, I'd win back her affections with a single question. "Want anything from the cafeteria?"

Her eyes would light up. "Coffee, light, with a splash of amaretto flavor, please."

"Uh-huh," I'd say. "Like yesterday."

It's not like Clarice and I did nothing. We did work. It's just that 37.5 hours was about twice as many hours as we needed to be in the office. I always said if you ever wanted to find us during the holidays, you needed only to look at the Quakerbridge Mall. Every time I dawdled by Lord & Taylor, there she was.

"Hello, boss," I'd say, my arms full of shopping bags in the middle of a business day.

"Merry Christmas!" she'd smile. "What do you think of this tie for my husband?"

For three years I worked at ETS, drawing a fine salary, covered by excellent insurance, taking paid vacations and loading up my 401(k). My first year I wrote more than 100 writing prompts and rubrics for inclusion in a new textbook, and I spent time in Virginia Beach working on the NAEP writing project. At the end of that year, I got a fat bonus and a nice raise. My second year I was the project director of the country's first *online* state assessment, and I spent a weekend in Fort Lauderdale leading a mini–scoring project made up of Florida teachers. At the end of that year, I got a fatter bonus and an unheard-of 25 percent raise. My third year I was involved in more experimental work, helping build automated systems that could edit prose for grammar, usage, and mechanics (like that damned Microsoft Word program that's always telling me how to pen sentences) and managing a *human* essay-scoring project that would ultimately lead to the creation of dozens of *computer* essay-scoring systems (like the ones we'd fantasized about in Iowa, years before). At the end of that year, due to the company's financial belt tightening, I got a moderate bonus and only a modicum of a raise.

So I quit. It wasn't the money, really, but a combination of things. First, I was bored to tears at ETS. Pretty much every day I read from one end of the Internet to the other: CNN.com, SI.com, ESPN.com, USSoccer.com, Salon.com, Slate.com, Nerve.com, Monster.com, before starting all over again. Second, given I had no interest in the testing business and no inclination to climb the company ladder, I had no reason to stay. I may have wanted a salary and health insurance, but I wasn't willing to give up the rest of my life for it. I still had the inkling I had a book or a theory of relativity gestating inside. And, third, I was just not a very good corporate soldier.

I hated the foolish rules that continued to be established by ETS management, the illogical things we were told to do for what seemed no good reason. I hated the two-hour meetings in which we accomplished all of five minutes' work; I hated the employee evaluations we wrote about *ourselves*, on which we were supposed to objectively assess the quality of our own work (to Clarice's dismay, in analyzing my own performance I checked off only the "superior" boxes); and I hated, especially, the electronic security system ETS had set up for every door, where we employees were supposed to flash our ID cards at the card reader before we entered or exited any building. While that might be a perfectly reasonable expectation of a company's employees, I found the idea maddening. At times I would walk up to a sliding door that was *already open*, and I was supposed *not* to walk through it—I was supposed to go to the wall and flash my ID before doing so, so someone could keep track of me. I was an independent New Englander, and having spent a lot of my youth in New Hampshire—the "Live Free or Die" state—I was most certainly not a proponent of any electronic surveillance system.

Plus, ETS's little security system was extra-bothersome because the company's campus was enormous, and I had to go through three buildings to get from my office to the cafeteria. That meant every day I went to get Clarice and me a cup of coffee, I was supposed to flash my badge to get out of my building, flash it again to get into the second building, again to get out of the second building, and finally one last time to get into the building that housed the cafeteria. Then I was supposed to turn around and do it all again on my return trip, that time while trying to juggle at least two steaming hot cups of coffee (if not a bagel, a cruller, perhaps a croissant).

Half the time I approached a sliding door, it would already be open, but my ETS colleagues wouldn't go through, lining up instead like lemmings in front of the open entrance, waiting to eagerly flash their badges at the electronic gatekeeper. Eventually, as a matter of dignity, I thought "#$%^& that," and I began to walk through every open door I saw. Sometimes I walked through doors I didn't even need to, just to be intransigent, loving the fact I was screwing with the system. Secretly

I hoped someone was checking our ID trails, because I liked to think of the charge of fear some militant, corporate security dude might feel one day when he saw I'd checked into my office at 9 A.M. and then checked out of another building, 500 yards away, four hours later.

"We've got a situation!" I imagined him screaming.

Ultimately, it wasn't even the security doors that finally made me quit, but the fund-raising drive. Every Christmas/ Hanukkah/Kwanzaa season, ETS did two things: it threw a big company party, and it raised money for the United Way. At the party, we ate mediocre meals, listened to tepid speeches, and feigned wonder about who would win the end-of-year bonuses when that cash was clearly destined to go to the corporate officers yet again. As for the fund-raising drive, while in my first year it had seemed like a gesture of goodwill, by my third year it was as generous as a forced march. The company seemed less interested in raising money for charity than it did in being able to claim 100 percent ETS employee participation in the program. When my donation wasn't sent to the ETS offices promptly enough in 2003, I received a terse communication from a company vice president. Her e-mail read:

> Todd—
> Our records indicate you have not yet made a contribution
> to the ETS Cares Campaign.
> Harriet

I had to give Harriet credit for the subtlety of her shake-down. She didn't demand I pay. She didn't insist I immediately write out a check. No, Harriet was too sly for that. She mentioned the company's "records." She wanted me to know a close eye was being kept on me and my kind.

Uh-uh, I thought. Any holiday donations I made were *my* business, not ETS's. I *wasn't* paying.

Instead, I quit. I was looking for a reason, and that was close enough. I wrote a resignation letter to Clarice, turned off the lights in my office, and shared some good laughs with colleagues at my farewell party (we all talked about my writing career as if it already existed, although I remained completely unpublished except for my stories on tests). After the party, I got in my Volkswagen and prepared to drive away, but before I did so, I pulled into the circular drive in front of my ETS building and I sped around and around the circle. With my tires squealing and my head out the window, I screamed, "So long, suckers!" to the friends who had gathered to wave good-bye. How we laughed.

Eventually pulling away from ETS, I was content, happy with my decision to leave that cushy job. My ETS experience had been fruitful, as it was there I'd gotten my first real job, and I'd succeeded at it, too. I had climbed to the top of the standardized testing industry, and when I didn't like the view, I had decided to climb down.

I just thought it was time for the rest of my life to begin.

Retirement

My Own Private Halliburton

B **Y MARCH 2005,** I'd been "retired" from ETS for a year and a half, but it had been a lucrative year and a half indeed. As soon as I'd hung up my ETS pencil, the offers for consulting work started flooding in, and those offers were not small. I accepted because I had to pay the bills (damn, that was some Cobra health payment!) *and* because I was unqualified to do anything else. I took gigs with former colleagues at ETS to develop training materials, with Maria (who was in business for herself in Iowa City) to write test items, and with Riverside Publishing in Chicago, which had mysteriously gotten my name and quickly signed me to a contract as a "test-scoring expert." A friend from NCS had also called to ask if I could lend a hand on a scoring project, but the pay was so small (17 bucks an hour) I had to make a serious effort not to laugh in my old pal's face.

Being a consultant was like running my own private Halliburton: I did what I felt like and charged what I wanted, the work characterized by high pay and low oversight. As an independent contractor, I took the jobs that interested me and said no to the ones that didn't. If I was unsure about a job, I usually made some exorbitant request for money, a number I fully expected would be refused, and more often than not I got an "OK" e-mailed back. By the spring of '05, I had a contract with Riverside Publishing to develop scoring systems, items, and rubrics for their WASL Goal 2 test (subject areas: Social Studies, Health & Fitness, and the Arts), and the amount they were paying was so shocking I made a point to drop the number into conversation with family and friends at every turn, as gauche as I knew that was. It was a ridiculous amount, and I knew for that price Riverside could've hired about 100 NCS scorers to do the work I alone had agreed to. Still, I signed the contract and took the money, deciding right then Riverside was my favorite employer ever.

In the spring of 2005, I agreed to travel to Phoenix for three months as an ETS representative, to provide scoring expertise for the 2005 NAEP science project. I'd been an NAEP science scorer in 1996, a trainer in 2000, and now in 2005 I was virtually "scorer emeritus," a highly paid consultant assisting ETS in overseeing the entire operation. My friend Olivia had retired from ETS, so she wasn't in charge anymore, but she would be in Phoenix for six weeks as a consultant. I was looking forward to the job, because it'd been almost five full years—since 2000 NAEP science—that I'd been on-site at a test-scoring project for any length of time, and I was interested to see if the work had become any less ridiculous than my previous experiences had led me to believe.

Before I flew from Princeton to Phoenix, I sat in on a conference call between ETS and NCS (actually, by that time NCS was known as NCS-Pearson or Pearson Education or Pearson Educational Measurement—I wasn't exactly sure because they changed aliases as often as a fleeing bank robber). I was on the call from my apartment, while on the line from the ETS's offices were Olivia and Kelly, the new director of NAEP science. A number of Pearson personnel were on the phone, too, some from Iowa City and some from Phoenix, and while introductions were made, I didn't get all of it. A name or two I recognized from my NCS past, but there were too many disembodied voices and unconnected names for it to make a lot of sense to me, so while I stayed on the call for its duration, I didn't really know who was talking at any one time.

The call was about logistics—hotels, flights, dates, the number of scorers hired, the number of items to be scored, deadlines, expectations—but before we wrapped up, a final discussion concerned a content issue. It was about an eight-grade earth science question, and somebody was trying to figure out what the correct answer really was. It wasn't an item I would be directly involved with, but I nonetheless listened to the conversation with considerable interest. Olivia's voice may have been the only one I recognized (that cheeky British accent), but I still found the dialogue an absolute delight.

Disembodied Voice: Olivia, this is the item about chemical reactions. The question asks the students to describe what happens when the liquid is added to the solid.

Olivia: Uh-huh.

Disembodied Voice: So the rubric says the correct answer is that the liquid *boils*.

Olivia: Right.

Disembodied Voice: Then why is Anchor Paper #7 not given credit?

Olivia: What's Anchor Paper #7 say?

Disembodied Voice: It says the liquid *sizzles*.

Olivia: *Sizzling* isn't *boiling*.

Disembodied Voice: It's not?

Second Disembodied Voice: Of course it is.

Olivia: Of course it isn't.

Disembodied Voice: Why not?

Olivia: *Sizzling* might happen to bacon. It doesn't happen to liquids. *Sizzling* is about sound, heat. That's not *boiling*, which is changing from liquid to gas.

Second Disembodied Voice: Is *sizzling* any different than *boiling* to an eighth grader?

Olivia: It should be.

Second Disembodied Voice: I don't see how we can expect those kids to know the difference.

Olivia: It's not hard.

Disembodied Voice: What about Practice Paper #9, then? It says the liquid *bubbles*.

Olivia: I'd accept that. Did we accept that?

Disembodied Voice: Yup.

Second Disembodied Voice: So yes to *bubbles* but no to *sizzles*.

Olivia: Right.

Second Disembodied Voice: I don't see the difference.

Third Disembodied Voice: Maybe we need to make a list.

Fourth Disembodied Voice: Good idea.

Olivia: Sure, let's do that.

Disembodied Voice: So right now, the liquid *boils* is accepted, but *sizzles* and *bubbles* are not.

Olivia: No. *Bubbles* and *boils* are accepted, but *sizzles* is not.

Disembodied Voice: Right.

Another Disembodied Voice: What about it *fizzes*?

Second Disembodied Voice: Fizzes or *fizzles*?

Third Disembodied Voice: Either.

Random Disembodied Voice: Well if we can't take *sizzles*, then I don't see how we can take *fizzes*.

Olivia: Hold on. *Fizzing* isn't the same as *sizzling*. It's not the same as *fizzling*, for that matter.

Second Disembodied Voice: Of course it is!

Olivia: No, if something *fizzles*, it means it is running out. Sputtering. If something *fizzes*, that's a chemical reaction, like *foaming*.

Disembodied Voice: Is *foaming* good?

Olivia: Yes, of course.

Second Disembodied Voice: No!

Disembodied Voice: No?

Olivia: Yes!

Random Disembodied Voice: Wait, what did we say about *fizzles* again?

Disembodied Voice: *Fizz-es* or *fizz-les*?

Olivia: Either.

Disembodied Voice: Both?

Olivia: No.

Disembodied Voice: I'm sorry, is *foams* acceptable or not?

{End of Scene}

The first thing I noticed on my first day at the Pearson scoring center in Phoenix was the intense emphasis on security. I don't mean on physical security, mind you, not the safety of the building or its employees. No, I mean *corporate* security. The building may have had locked doors you could only get through with a picture ID, but even more serious than keeping people out was Pearson's intention to keep secret everything going on *inside* those doors. On the building's main entrance was a sign prohibiting all cameras and recording equipment from the site, and the first thing one saw when passing through that door was a bold announcement proclaiming "Camera Phones Will Be Confiscated." Additionally, the Pearson scorers had to sit through a lengthy human resources orientation that first day, and it included both the signing of confidentiality agreements promising to keep mum about the company's inner workings *and* a discussion on how to deal with intrusive media types who might be snooping around ("Immediately contact the site manager!").

I said to Olivia, "It's getting to be like Vegas around here. What happens at Pearson stays at Pearson."

The second thing I noticed was the scorers themselves, and as Kelly and I stood by the center's front door, we watched in awe the procession of temporary employees filing in. While the scorers who populate the Pearson sites around the country where I'd worked had never been notably youthful, energetic, attractive, intelligent, or even "normal," this Phoenix parade included (among some number of average Joes and Janes) an aged guy pushing his way through the door with a walker, his lunchbox delicately perched between the handles as he crept slowly forward. Behind him was an Indian woman in full sari; a guy in a wheelchair; two white-haired women, holding between them a recent piece of needlework; an albino kid, eerily white haired and entirely without pigment; a morbidly obese dude whose enormous pants only stayed up over his massive waist due to some cable-sized suspenders, his belly so wide he had to turn sideways to even get through the door; a woman wearing a surgical mask, à la Michael Jackson on a shopping spree; a fellow in a full safari outfit, khaki pants and khaki vest, and even a pith helmet atop his head; another albino (seriously, what are the odds?), this one somehow not seeming as completely colorless as his predecessor but no less unnerving; an elderly African American man in shiny, pointy-toed shoes and a dapper zoot suit, a black fedora perched jauntily atop his silver curls; an unfortunate reddish guy whose skin seemed to be peeling right off his scalp and arms; a fellow, in the 100+ degree Arizona heat, wearing a wool blazer and an Irish driving cap pulled low over his eyes; and a guy carrying under his arm, into his first day of work, a George Foreman grill, the family-sized one.

I leaned close to Kelly, whispering. "I give to you the backbone of the standardized testing industry."

She shook her head. "The uglies and unhirables are back."

By 2005, the NAEP test had changed a bit. For years, ETS had been the U.S. government's sole contractor to develop and administer the NAEP tests, with ETS subcontracting the job of actually *scoring* the student responses to Pearson. By 2005, ETS and Pearson were cocontractors with the U.S. government, meaning Pearson was no longer in a role subservient to ETS. Therefore, when it was time to score the NAEP science responses in Phoenix in 2005, both Pearson and ETS personnel were on site to manage the project. We representatives of ETS were really only there in an advisory role. We were supposed to ensure continuity by helping Pearson staffers if they had any questions about content decisions made in previous years.

In that role, Olivia and I began the NAEP science project sitting in a large office at the Phoenix site, drinking coffee and reading *USA Today* as we waited for questions from the Pearson trainers. No questions occurred, however, and for days we didn't hear from anyone. Eventually Olivia got bored and started walking into the many cubicles filled with computers and scorers, and she began to find plenty of problems. The Pearson people may not have been bringing us their questions, but they also weren't getting a lot done. Mostly those trainers were failing their Trend Tests, and although they were failing to make any progress, they still had no inclination to ask those of us from ETS for help.

"They're getting our help," Olivia said, "whether they want it or not. There are four teams in real trouble, so you assist groups 8 and 10, and I'll take 1 and 4."

Although the first week of the project was nearly over, neither group 8 nor group 10 had passed a Trend Test at all (remember, a Trend Test compared the scores given by a 2005 team to the scores given by a 2000 team on the *same* student responses). Groups 8 and 10 had each gone through training and then failed their tests, before retraining and refailing them again and again for the rest of the week. Because neither team had passed a single Trend Test, neither group had begun scoring the student responses from 2005, so it was as if their first week of work hadn't even happened. Both groups were spinning their wheels, and when I visited each cubicle, the teams looked completely defeated: the scorers looked addled and the trainers lost.

Group 10 had the easier items, but the bigger problem was their trainer. Burt was an elderly gent who'd recently retired from a long career as an engineer, and while there was no question about Burt's brain, there was certainly some question about his training abilities. After his team would fail a Trend Test, Burt would have his 10 befuddled scorers gather around his computer to look at the disagreements between scores, and then he—in what was generally the worst training maneuver I ever saw—would completely exacerbate his scorers' misunderstandings by claiming it was all too confusing to figure out.

"This is crazy," he'd say to his group. "I don't know what those scorers in 2000 were doing!"

"What does this rubric mean?" Burt would demand. "I can't imagine what those idiots at ETS were thinking!"

"Look at this response," he'd exclaim, pointing at his screen. "How could they have given this a 4 when it's clearly a 2?"

Then someone might point at the screen for him, "No, Burt, *they* gave it a 2, and one of our people gave it the 4."

"Never mind," he'd mutter.

At the end of those edifying review sessions, Burt would have his group take another Trend Test, and more often than not his group would suffer an even more ignominious failure. Because Burt's idea of retraining seemed focused not at all on content issues but mostly on pointing fingers and avoiding blame, that his group would fail consistently wasn't particularly surprising. Although I tried to give Burt tips on scoring correctly and advice on dealing with confused scorers, the old geezer was not very receptive at all—he didn't know who I was or where I'd come from, and, damn it, he'd been an engineer! Burt knew *everything* about science, so he continued to ignore my advice and his group continued to fail its Trend Tests.

Instead, I concentrated my efforts on group 8. I told myself Burt's unwillingness to listen made working with group 10 pointless, but the more truthful reason I settled in with group 8 was the crush I had on its trainer, Hailey. Given the option of working with a grumpy old man who ignored me and a beautiful, young woman who took my suggestions to heart, there was very little question what I would do: I stopped dealing with Burt almost entirely and pretty much moved right into the cubicle with Hailey's group 8.

Hailey's team, unfortunately, was having as hard a time as Burt's was, although at least they had a good reason: group 8 was doing a linked item, seven questions in a row about pendulums. That meant group 8 didn't have to pass one Trend Test to qualify to start scoring the 2005 items—they had to pass *seven* of them, one each for questions 1, 2, 3, 4, 5, 6, and 7. Hailey's task, in other words, was seven times harder than Burt's.

I didn't know a lot about pendulums, but one night in my hotel room I spent the entire evening reviewing the items, rubrics, and training papers for the pendulum items, and by morning I was completely versed on how to score them. Scoring tests, it should be said, isn't about being an expert in a subject area—it's about understanding how to classify student responses. That was my area of expertise. By the next morning, I knew as little about pendulums as ever, but I was absolutely certain how to score the student responses written about them.

Group 8 had 10 scorers, each plopped in front of a computer. In the front row sat two, aging hippy women who smelled like patchouli and giggled like schoolgirls. Next to them was Art, a nattily dressed fellow who was taking a break from his job as a used car salesman. In the back row, closest to me and Hailey, was a portly little accountant who had been newly laid off from his real job, a guy who belted his huge pants halfway up his enormous pot belly and kept looking over our shoulders at whatever Hailey and I were doing. Next to him was a youngish guy who looked a little freaky, and though he spent all his free time drawing comic books, he was dressed from head to toe in black, wearing army boots and an overcoat as if part of Columbine's Trench Coat Mafia.

I admit group 8 did try hard. They tried to listen to Hailey's training and make sense of it. But the pendulum items were linked, so those scorers had to understand and apply seven rubrics at the same time, *and* those seven rubrics were constantly changing: whatever answer a student gave for question 1 affected what their correct answer would be for question 2, right on down the line to 7, so the group 8 scorers had to keep adjusting their ideas about when an answer was right and when it was wrong. While I managed to figure out the scoring pretty quickly (based in large part on my years of experience), I could still admit the pendulum questions were a bit complex for those relatively new scorers.

Even conceding the pendulum questions were hard, I still couldn't come up with an explanation for those scorers not understanding how to score the items *a week* after the training had begun. It had taken me one evening to figure it all out, and Hailey had it mastered, too. Plus, the Comic Book Guy in the back row—who turned out to be less a scary gunman than sweet artist—had absolutely no trouble scoring the student responses correctly. It was his teammates who were at a complete loss. The aging hippies in the front row seemed completely baffled by the scoring (were they getting stoned at break?), and while the dapper Art continued to put wrong scores on the student responses, he also kept explaining his bad decisions in a mellifluous baritone, just the smooth-talking bullshit you'd expect from a used car salesman. There was no score, no matter how incorrect, Art wouldn't defend to his dying breath. The Fat Accountant in the back row was doing the same thing, both scoring wrong *and* arguing about it.

"But I'm a mathematician," he'd insist in defense of his scores, even when he was the only one of 10 who had doled out an incorrect number.

Some of the rules that ETS and Pearson had established weren't helping matters, either. For instance, our group had to pass all seven Trend Tests at the same time, so if the group passed the tests for questions 1 through 6 but failed it on question 7, the whole process had to be repeated, and all seven tests had to be taken again. In those cases, the scorers would sit around for about an hour as Hailey got feedback to retrain them, and then after retraining/contentious debating, the group would take the tests again. If on the second try the group passed question 7 but failed any of the 1 through 6 they had just passed, it was back to the drawing board for a third try. For days this went on—testing and mostly passing but retraining and then testing again and mostly passing while still failing a test previously passed—and by the end of the project's second week group 8 had still never passed all seven Trend Tests at the same time. They had still not qualified to begin the scoring of the 2005 responses, which was the actual purpose of the project. Some days the group would pass an item like question 1 five straight times (clearly indicating the group's understanding of how to score it), but then when 1 was the *only* item they didn't pass on the team's sixth try, that was enough to consider the entire effort a failure and to necessitate a seventh retesting.

Both Hailey and I were beginning to get considerably frustrated. Whenever she and I scored student responses as part of the Trend Tests, *we* were getting high reliabilities, so there was no question the factor hurting us most was the group 8 scorers themselves. They were just not getting it, except for Comic Book Guy.

"We should let Comic Book Guy score all the responses," Hailey joked.

It was the very thought that had been rattling through my head. I realized it was simply a matter of percentages: to pass the tests we needed to get more good scores in the system, and fewer bad ones. While we could fantasize that would happen with the improvement of group 8's scorers, that clearly wasn't happening. Instead, Hailey and I decided to front-load the statistics, and the next time group 8 took the Trend Tests, she and I (although supervisors and trainers were not supposed to score responses), with the help of Comic Book Guy, scored half of the student responses needed to run a Trend Test. After we'd done that—when the reliabilities for all seven of those items were good and high—we allowed the remaining nine scorers to score responses, too, and even their general incompetence wasn't bad enough to ruin the overall statistics. We passed all seven tests.

"Success!" Hailey yelled as the group celebrated, the scorers (except for Comic Book Guy) under the dubious impression that they'd finally figured it all out.

Having at last "passed" the Trend Tests, group 8 was finally "qualified" to start scoring the student responses from 2005. The group was greatly relieved, as was the management of both Pearson and ETS.

"Good work," the Pearson scoring director, John, told Hailey and me. "Now we can really get busy scoring the current year work"

Not exactly. Although group 8 had finally passed the Trend Tests and was considered qualified to score 2005 responses, the problem remained that we'd have to continue to pass the Trend Tests again and again. Although my experience in testing had led me to believe one didn't forget how to score an item over even a weekend's time (you could have woken me up on that project, in the middle of a night after I'd pounded 10 beers,

and I still could've immediately told you how to score the pendulum items), in the infinite wisdom of the industry's higher-
ups, it'd been decided any time a team stopped scoring for
more than 30 minutes, they had to again pass the Trend Tests.
That meant group 8 had to take and pass the tests at the start
of each new day, and even more maddeningly they had to pass
the tests a second time each day after breaking for their half-
hour lunch.

"Are you kidding?" I asked John. "Someone thinks we're
going to forget how to score at lunchtime?"

"Psychometricians," he told me. "What can you do?"

It was completely illogical and a waste of time. Some mornings it would take us a good three and a half hours to even pass
the Trend Tests the first time (and that usually involved statistical manipulation), so we'd only score the 2005 responses for
about 30 minutes before it was time for lunch. After lunch, of
course, we were then supposed to pass the tests *again*, which
usually involved another two or three hours of training, retraining, arm twisting, verbal abuse, concession, and maybe cheating. Only then could we spend another 60 minutes or so
actually scoring the 2005 responses before the day came to a
close. It was ridiculous to have to retake the Trend Tests after
every 30-minute break—labor-intensive and exhausting and
frustrating to all involved—but it was a process we nonetheless
repeated daily.

"Well," Hailey scoffed, "if they're so obsessed with these
30-minute breaks, we should take 29-minute lunches instead."

She must have been a seer, because no sooner had Hailey
made that joke than Pearson and ETS made a combined
announcement about breaks: no more 30-minute lunches.
Instead, it was collaboratively decided to change the daily
work schedule, and rather than the scorers taking two 15-
minute breaks and one 30-minute lunch each day, the scorers would forthwith take three 20-minute breaks. Or, frankly,

the individual groups could come up with any schedule they wanted, providing they took 60 minutes' worth of breaks each day but *no* rests of 30 minutes or more.

Such a schedule, of course, meant each group would only have to pass their Trend Tests once a day, in the morning, but not a second time after lunch. That change was welcomed by all, because the new schedule freed everyone up from the hassles of a second test while allowing us to concentrate on the real job at hand, scoring the 2005 responses. The plan was utterly ingenious, this anything-less-than-30-minutes-for-lunch schedule, a diabolical ruse cleverly devised by Pearson and ETS to circumvent the rules previously established by, well, Pearson and ETS.

"Is this really how we're handling this?" I asked John. "You don't want to waive the silly twice-a-day Trend Tests instead of taking ridiculously abbreviated breaks?"

"Can't do that," he said. "Rules are rules."

Rules being rules, Hailey and I conceded the point, and we established that group 8 would take a daily lunch break of exactly 29 minutes and 55 seconds. We told our scorers to go ahead and make up those missing five seconds on either their morning or afternoon break, but we also warned them not to be even the tiniest bit delayed when coming back from lunch. Another five seconds after that 29-minute, 55-second lunch, we advised, and they would be in very real danger of forgetting all they knew about scoring the pendulum items. Given the precision of the work they were already doing, the very exact and scientific nature of it, that was not a risk Hailey and I were willing to take.

By the time the project was halfway over, I left group 8 in Hailey's capable hands and began to train items myself. Although I hadn't originally been scheduled to, a number of Pearson trainers were having enough difficulty that Olivia thought it would be a good idea. Burt, the crotchety coot from group 10, had been the biggest problem, and his groups had barely accomplished any work. Burt couldn't get his team to agree with each other when scoring, and he couldn't get them to agree with the groups from 2000, and as much as Burt blamed everyone else for that—bad items! bad rubrics! busted computers!—Olivia and I thought the problem might be good ol' Burt himself.

"Seriously," I said to John, the Pearson scoring director, "has his team *ever* passed Trend? Have they finished scoring even a single item?"

"Well," John answered, "you know the notes we got from ETS haven't been very helpful in clarifying the scoring issues and . . . ." It was interesting for me to hear these complaints, because in my many years at Pearson (née NCS) in Iowa City, we'd been coached always to defer to ETS. We temporary employees had been told to concede to whatever the Princeton company wanted; in those days, Pearson had to answer to ETS, and hence we did whatever they said. In Phoenix in 2005, now that Pearson was no longer ETS's underling, the dynamic had clearly changed. I saw for the first time that if things went wrong, Pearson was perfectly willing to point the finger at ETS, to lay the blame directly at the feet of its cocontractor/competitor. Pearson's attitude seemed to be if there was going to be an NAEP fall guy, it wasn't going to be Pearson.

Olivia was having none of it. "That's baloney," she said. "Burt is obviously a terrible trainer. If he couldn't finish that single astronomy item, he's just bad. Let Todd train it."

"That astronomy item is simple," I agreed. "It's *one* item! *Three* points! It's almost incomprehensible to me his team couldn't do it. How long did they work on it anyway?"

John hesitated a bit. "Not really Burt's fault . . . ," he began, before Olivia and I basically shouted him down. "I guess they spent a week on it," John said.

"A week? A bloody week for a three-point item?" Olivia shook her head.

"OK," John conceded, and it was decided I would retrain Burt's failed astronomy item with a new group of scorers. John didn't seem thrilled, and I got the feeling he didn't necessarily want me to succeed—my success would indicate the problem was his Pearson trainer, not ETS.

Olivia and I were telling the ETS higher-ups the reason Burt's team had failed to pass Trend for the astronomy item was because Burt was a bad trainer. Meanwhile, John and his people were claiming the responsibility for Burt's failure had to be taken by ETS, because Pearson was saying the rubric was bad and the student responses from 2000 had been mis-scored. By the time I got around to training the item, there was a lot on the line. Both ETS and Pearson were eager to see who was really at fault.

Before I started the training, John asked if I wanted "slow but accurate" scorers to work on the astronomy item or if I wanted "fast but not-so-accurate" ones. It wasn't an unreasonable question, because one of the things we were always considering was both getting the items scored and having the deadlines met. Still, John's question was a tacit admission Pearson was employing a bunch of "not-so-accurate" scorers. When I asked John to clarify if his question meant Pearson knew they had employees on site who were incorrectly scoring student responses that would ultimately make up the "Nation's Report Card," he claimed ignorance.

"Only kidding," John said, starting to walk away. "I just wanted to say you can begin the retraining tomorrow morning."

Pearson, I thought.

Of course, ETS—the company whose side I was now on in this Battle of the Industry Bigwigs—wasn't completely pure of heart itself. The afternoon before, on the daily conference call between those of us in Phoenix and the home offices in Iowa City and Princeton, I had confidently announced I anticipated no problem when rescoring Burt's astronomy item. I said I'd read the item and rubric and I'd studied the training papers, and I fully expected to pass the Trend Test on our first try and to score all the 2005 responses within half a day. It was really a simple item, I announced, child's play for a trainer of my experience and expertise.

Linda, the ETS psychometrician in Princeton, seemed less enthusiastic about my confidence than I would have expected. "Don't do too good a job scoring it," she said over the phone. "Someone's going to have to match your reliability in 2009."

"You're saying 'Don't do too good a job' scoring this item?" I asked.

"That's not our official stance, of course," Linda paused. "I'm just saying don't go overboard. Maybe use some of the less good scorers if you think it's that easy."

Her request was no more shocking than John's question previously had been. I knew that Lydia had to take a long-term view of the project, so she cared more about getting a reliability number that could be easily matched in four years than she did about the correct scores getting put on the papers.

ETS, I thought.

Regardless of the fact Pearson gave me some of the "not-so-accurate" variety of scorers to work on the astronomy item, and regardless of the fact ETS wasn't rooting for me to do "too good a job" on it, and regardless of the fact that Burt's group had spent an entire week working unsuccessfully on the question (approximately 500 man-hours that resulted in the passing of zero Trend Tests and the scoring of zero 2005 student responses), my retraining went exactly as I predicted: I trained the item, we passed the Trend Test on our first try, and three hours later we had successfully scored all 2,400 of the 2005 student responses, with the group's reliability settling in at a robust (but not too robust) 90 percent. It went so well we didn't even need to doctor any stats.

The question was a three-pointer asking why the Earth got dark each night, with the correct answer being because our planet rotates on its axis. The rubric assigned scores of 3, 2, and 1 based on whether the response showed complete understanding, partial understanding, or no understanding of that concept. In theory it was a perfectly clear way to score, although I could see where an inexperienced trainer/scorer like Burt might have difficulties. The student responses were nowhere near as clear as the rubric imagined, and confusion could have resulted from the many discrete answers. The students didn't all say it got dark each night "because our planet rotates on its axis." No, they said every possible variation of that, including the vague "because our planet rotates," the wrong-but-in-the-right-ballpark "because our planet rotates around the sun," and the plain-irrelevant "because the sun rotates on its axis." Given all the "rotating" going on in the student responses, all the "spinning" and "turning" and "twirling," some of it of the Earth and some of the sun (not to mention an occasional moon), I could definitely see where it'd gone wrong for Burt's group.

It didn't go wrong for mine, though. I started the training by grandiloquently touting the skills of my group, telling them the bald-faced lie that we'd brought them together into this "super team" because they were the best scorers in the building. As they giggled proudly at that, I launched immediately into the training.

"The question is why does the Earth get dark each night," I began, "and the answer, of course, ..."

That was where I pulled off the first of my training tricks. I had discovered only the previous week that the Earth got dark each night "because it spun on its axis," when I Googled the topic. But by saying "of course" that was the answer, I made it seem like information everyone should know. That was important, because I wanted that team to think I was the authority on all things science, and with some linguistic confidence I'd pulled it off. Those 20 people knew little about me (really, only that I worked at ETS and was from "back east"), and I needed them to assume I was some kind of genius—it would make everything else I told them during the training seem like scientific gospel.

"The answer, *of course*, is because the Earth rotates on its axis." I nodded my head up and down, smiling and making eye contact that signaled "Right?" My people nodded back, completely acquiescing to whatever I said. They stared at me like I was an oracle, as I'd hoped. When I had seen Burt train, he'd acted weak, showing his team confusing responses he didn't know how to score, confessing his occasional ignorance about how the rubric worked, and claiming bewilderment about which answers were right or wrong. To a group of confused employees, Burt had acted confused. I, conversely, was acting like I had all the answers, like scoring the astronomy item was the simplest thing I could imagine.

And my team of suckers was buying it.

"'Because the Earth rotates/spins/twirls *on its axis*' gets a 3," I told them. "Right?" They nodded.

"'Because the Earth rotates/spins/twirls/orbits *around the sun*' gets a 2," I told them, "for at least understanding the darkness results from some relationship between the two. OK?" They nodded.

"'Because *the sun* rotates/spins/twirls on its axis' gets only a 1," I told them, "because we don't care about the sun rotating." They nodded.

For emphasis, and for my own amusement, I reiterated that point. "Remember, we don't give a damn about *the sun* rotating. Not a damn."

Next we looked at the Anchor Papers, and they clearly exemplified the rules I'd explained. Most of the 20 people in the group seemed to grasp the classifications we were making, although three or four of them looked befuddled. I thought I'd give them one more chance.

"Before we begin scoring Practice Papers," I said, "is everyone clear on how we are scoring?" Many of the people nodded, but some did not. A few of them had guilty looks on their faces, as if they *thought* they should understand but still didn't.

A red-haired woman meekly raised her hand and asked a question. "I'm sorry, but could you repeat again what the deal is with 'rotates'? Or 'spins' or 'twirls' or whatever? When is that good and when is it bad?"

"Sure," I said. "Remember what the correct answer really is. The Earth gets dark every night because the planet rotates on its axis, turning part of it away from the light of the sun, right?" I loved Google.

Looking down, the Redhead nodded. "But how's that different from the 'Earth rotates' or 'rotates around the sun'?"

"Two things happen here," I said, clearly remembering the diagram I had seen on the Internet. "One, the Earth rotates on its axis, and, two, the Earth orbits/rotates around the sun. Distinct things, right?"

The Redhead neither looked up nor nodded. I noticed a couple of other people avoiding my gaze also, indicating their uncertainty, too.

"OK," I said, "how about a quick diagram?" Grabbing a magic marker and a whiteboard, I re-created the Internet image. I drew a big sun in the middle of the board, and I drew arrows showing a smaller Earth orbiting/rotating around that sun. I also drew the Earth slightly tilted, with arrows showing how it spun around like a top on its own axis. Proudly I showed the group my drawing, but it didn't necessarily look like it helped. A couple of faces, including the Redhead's, were scrunched up in concentration and apparent bewilderment. I realized I wasn't the greatest artist, but c'mon.

I refused to give up. She *would* understand. They all would. I grabbed the scorer sitting close to me. "Stand here," I said. "OK, people, look. Barry here is the sun, and I'm the Earth."

First I spun in place. "I'm the Earth rotating on its axis, right?" They all nodded, the Redhead included.

Next I walked around Barry. "Now I'm the Earth rotating/ orbiting the sun, right?" They all nodded, the Redhead included.

And finally, I walked around Barry while also spinning on my own axis. Frankly, it was a little dizzying, but I pulled it off. "Now I'm the Earth spinning on its axis while also rotating/ orbiting the sun, right? And remember, the Earth gets dark at night because it rotates on its axis, not because it rotates around the sun!" They all nodded, the Redhead included.

"I get it!" she said, my 3D reenactment of the Milky Way finally clarifying things for her.

The group quickly scored the Practice Papers so we could review them together, and most of the team grasped our scoring rules just fine. There may have been some confusion with pronouns ("Is this 'it' the Earth? Or the sun? Maybe it's the moon?") and their antecedents ("Wait, what's rotating here, anyway?")—not to mention the regular confusion about orbiting versus spinning—but the Practice Papers were still mostly scored correctly. Each time I asked an individual to explain what score he or she had given to a student response, for the most part he or she had scored it correctly, and for the most part the group agreed. We made it through the first nine papers without any real problems.

"Aaron, read Practice Paper #9, and tell us what you gave it, please," I instructed.

"The response says 'cuz the sun spins,' and I gave it a 1," he said.

"Why?"

"Because we don't give a damn about the rotation of the *sun*."

"Not a damn!" I smiled. "Very good." My people were *so* smart.

Well, not all of them. Darita, the woman in a sari whom I'd first seen on the project's first day, six weeks before, was having some troubles. When I asked her to read and score Practice Paper #10, she didn't seem to understand my request. Although as a group we had reviewed Practice Papers #1 through #9, Darita didn't seem to follow the procedure. I thought that was odd, since it was the same procedure every trainer was supposed to undertake for every item. Also, if anyone had been sitting in our cubicle for the last 10 minutes, it was pretty self-explanatory what was going on.

"Darita, please read and score #10," I said, and she responded by holding up her computer mouse toward me.

"No," I said. "Read and score #10 please." She held up the mouse *pad*.

I couldn't help it, and I smiled. "No," I said. "Paper #10." That time Darita actually put aside the packet of Practice Papers she held in one hand to pick up her scoring rubric, which she then waved to me. While I conceded it was pretty funny this apparent non-English speaker had already survived six weeks of the scoring project, I did get a little annoyed, too. I wanted the item to be scored correctly, and I didn't see how Darita was going to help in that regard. Turning to the scoring supervisor in charge of the group, I quietly asked if she was always like that.

"She barely speaks English," he said, "but she scores so incredibly slowly it doesn't matter. She can't screw anything up, so John said let her keep scoring."

That admission surprised me not at all, so I decided to skip Darita in my training and instead asked the dreaded Redhead beside her to read and score Practice Paper #10. After much hemming and hawing, and after considerable debate with herself, the Redhead announced her score for that response.

"OK, it says 'because the Earth orbits,'" she read. "Uh, I guess I'd give it a . . . I'd give it a 4."

I raised an eyebrow. Around the cubicle, interest was suddenly piqued. A number of the scorers picked up their heads to have a good look at her.

"A 4, you say?"

The Redhead was shaking her head up and down, at first mildly but then with more confidence. "Yup, a 4."

"Interesting," I said.

She looked at me expectantly, eager as a schoolchild, hoping she got it right. At that point, the scorer beside her (not Darita) kindly leaned in and whispered something.

"Wait, I don't mean a 4," the Redhead exclaimed. "I mean, I know it can't be a 4 . . . ."

I said nothing, and the Redhead stared down at the paper in front of her. Again she started to debate with herself, out loud ("It's the Earth that matters, not the sun, and there's no mention of the moon, but orbiting is the same as spinning"), as the group listened. At various times she mentioned the response might be a 3, a 2, a 1, but she never quite got around to deciding.

"So?" I asked.

"I'm gonna say it's . . . a . . . 3. Yes, a 3," she said.

The correct answer was actually a 2, but I didn't complain too loudly about the Redhead's guess of 3 because she *was* making progress of a sort. I mean, her second choice of 3 was at least theoretically possible; her original choice of 4 never would have worked because there wasn't even a 4 button to click on the computer.

"Well, 3 is wrong," I said to her. "But you are getting warmer."

Ultimately, neither Darita nor the Redhead had any long-term negative effect on our work. Darita pretty much sat quietly, barely scoring any responses, while the Redhead got shipped off to another project before she could screw up too mightily on mine. Given her problems, I wasn't sad to see the

Redhead go, and I figured she was probably getting transferred to a group where she would do less damage.

Wrong again.

The Redhead was actually reassigned to be part of the group scoring the SAT essays. It was the first year the SAT had included a writing section, and I'd wondered how those essays would be scored. I imagined, given the enormity and importance of that test, there had to be some cadre of teaching professionals reading the responses. I thought maybe there was some lab somewhere doing something academic and scientific to those writing samples, something other than putting them through the usual Pearson wringer. I should have known better.

Nonetheless, with the Redhead gone nothing could stop my team, and three hours after I had begun training, we were finished with the item. My group had passed our Trend Test (first try!) and successfully scored all the 2005 student responses (90 percent agreement!). After a week, Burt's team had scored zero responses; after three hours, my team had scored them all. My team and I sat back in our chairs, feeling smug and satisfied. Not only had we successfully scored the responses, but we'd finish the item quickly enough that we wouldn't have to take a Trend Test the next morning. We all felt great, at least until John popped into the cubicle. He saw us lounging and asked what we were doing, and when I smiled haughtily and told him we'd successfully scored the item already, John blanched. He told us we couldn't be done already. He said we had to run at least two Trend Tests for the results to matter.

"But we passed the Trend Test," I said. "and then we scored the 2005 responses quickly and accurately. Our reliability was 90 percent. Maybe you don't understand, John, but we are completely done with the scoring already."

"No, *you* don't understand," John replied. "You have to run at least two Trends, or the statistics don't count."

"But we never had any 30-minute break," I said. "I made sure we finished today so there would be no need for a Trend Test tomorrow morning."

"Doesn't matter," he said. "You must have two Trend Tests."

"So, what—you want us to take one now, retroactively?" I asked.

"I guess so."

"And what if we fail the test, after we've already finished the scoring?"

John shrugged. "I guess we'd have to dump the results and score the item again."

"You're saying you'd dump the correct scores already on those student responses to make us jump through some administrative hoop?"

"Rules are rules," he said.

Working in Theory

IF MY NEED for easy money meant I kept returning to the testing industry, that didn't mean I thought the business made any more sense. After NAEP science in 2005, I was more convinced than ever the scoring of open-ended test questions was a dubious proposition at best, and as I began to spend more time writing questions and passages, I began to see other problems in the industry, too. For instance, the emphasis on "bias and sensitivity" in the development of tests was an issue I thought clearly lacked standardization, and it seemed to me it often lacked common sense as well.

I don't doubt the value of bias and sensitivity concerns in the development of standardized tests, if only because those guidelines help to ensure that all students—regardless of gender, race, religion, or culture—have an equal opportunity to answer a test's questions correctly. Simply being aware of the possibility of bias and sensitivity issues means test makers don't

write questions only a certain population can answer. They don't
write questions in German, because then only speakers of that
Teutonic language could answer; they don't write questions anymore about "regattas," because there are only so many scions
of aristocratic, sailing families in the test-taking population these
days; and they don't write questions that are racist or sexist, or
are disparaging to any particular religion/nation/culture/
subculture/sub-subculture (we can't be hurting anyone's feelings now), or are focused on any topic that might be disturbing
or upsetting or even the slightest bit unsettling to the delicate
student population (because having to face up to the realities of
the world might be so discombobulating, little Billy or Mary—
or Jose or Paulita, DeShawn or LaKeesha, Hideki or Chidori,
Jagdeep or Amita—might not be able to concentrate enough
on the vitally important test in front of them).

But it seemed to me obsessing over those guidelines could
be something of a slippery slope, and it was a slope that I
thought we slid down too often. While conceding some topics
definitely needed to be avoided on tests (mature topics like sex
and drugs, controversial topics like abortion or the war in Iraq),
I didn't always understand my instructions to ignore others.
Writing test questions for one Department of Education, I was
given an item-writing guide that began by prohibiting anything
droll from being put on the test. "Avoid humor," the guide
cautioned. While I was surprised to read that warning, I was
grateful to have been given it because I might otherwise have
written a question or story that included something funny—up
to that point I'd been completely unaware of the potential danger to children of all things comical.

The item-writing guide continued by explaining that while
I could write about "music," I certainly couldn't mention "rap"
or "rock-and-roll"; and while I couldn't write about "dance,"
"ballet" itself was a most welcome topic. The guide further
steered me away from other speculative topics like "evolution"

and the notoriously offensive "holidays," especially "birthdays." When I boorishly asked what the problem was with birthdays, I was told dismissively that because Jehovah's Witnesses didn't believe in them, the DOE couldn't have a question including a cake and candles because it might throw some poor, little Witness into a tizzy.

I once sat in a meeting where we were instructed by a company's head of bias/sensitivity (a woman approaching retirement) that at no point could we include on any test a story about soccer. "No questions about sports," Doris said. "Girls don't know anything about sports."

One of my colleagues laughed aloud. Amber was in her 20s and was new to the company, but she'd also gone to college on an athletic scholarship.

"Ever hear of Title IX?" Amber asked, alluding to the federal law that had dramatically increased female participation in high school and college athletics. "Ever hear of Mia Hamm? Brandi Chastain?"

It was already a couple of years after the U.S. women's soccer team had dramatically won the 1999 Women's World Cup, when at the Rose Bowl in Pasadena more than 90,000 people— including the president of the United States—watched our women defeat the Chinese in a penalty-kick shootout to bring home the trophy. A *Sports Illustrated* cover shot of Chastain after she'd scored the winning goal—having ripped off her U.S. jersey, her chest covered only with a sports bra and her face covered with absolute glee—had been a matter of considerable conversation for years.

"Never heard of them," Doris said.

Another colleague chimed in. Alana was maybe 50 years old, but she hadn't been living with her head in the sand and hence knew something about the changing American landscape. "Plenty of girls know something about sports," she said. "And regardless, this story stands alone. One can correctly answer the questions simply by *reading* the story. There's no need for any previous knowledge about soccer."

"Girls don't know anything about sports," Doris said, her decision final.

So whenever I wrote test passages and questions, I always had to be aware of issues of bias and sensitivity (issues both real and imagined). I knew nothing even remotely controversial could ever come anywhere near those standardized tests. Even if that made for less interesting tests or less historically accurate tests, that's what I had to do. Since I wanted to get paid, that's exactly what I did: I sucked it up and wrote 'em down. For instance, after I spent a week researching the absolutely captivating tale of the Lewis and Clark expedition, I wrote a 1,000-word story about their adventure for a ninth-grade test. The account I turned in, of course, was a bit Disney-esque, the story of these earnest scientists/explorers trekking across the American continent, making friends with the Indian tribes they met (excuse me, the "Native American" tribes) while they mapped the countryside and catalogued newly discovered flora and fauna. It was a feel-good story, perfect for a Saturday morning cartoon.

And while my Lewis and Clark story was true, it was not completely forthcoming about the adventurers' real saga. My story failed to mention Lewis and Clark's Corps of Discovery was an expedition made up entirely of soldiers, heavily armed men willing to risk their lives to go places no white man (excuse me, "Caucasian") had ever trod, men who were at times violent and greedy, drunk and horny. My story failed to mention when the Corps of Discovery was threatened by the Lakota Sioux in South Dakota, it was only the sword of Captain Clark held up against a chief's throat that guaranteed their safe passage. It failed to mention Captain Lewis one morning gunning down two Blackfeet warriors who were trying to steal his horses, one of the Indians lying dead on the ground with a peace medal hanging from his neck that Lewis had proffered the night before. It failed to mention the soldiers' daily rations included both a pop of whiskey and a handful of tobacco. It failed to mention when in the Pacific Northwest, the Corps of Discovery eschewed eating the copious amounts of salmon to be found to instead dine on a diet of dogs they killed after purchasing them from local tribes. And my account failed to mention Captain Lewis's medical expertise repeatedly being brought to bear over the course of the expedition to deal with the incessant outbreaks of venereal disease from which the soldiers suffered, a problem resulting from their fraternization with the natives and, perhaps, one another.

Of all these fascinating aspects of Lewis and Clark's adventure, my story said not a word. Not a single word. It went without saying I couldn't include any of those true facts in my passage—nary a mention of the violence or the liquor, the dog dining or the intercultural sex swaps—so I didn't include them. If that meant the students weren't getting the full story, that's what it meant. I still turned in the passage, though, because the company wanted their story and I wanted my 500 bucks, so I guess it all worked out in the end.

In the world of standardized testing, the rubrics are the sacred scrolls. It is on those documents most experts believe standardized test scoring hinges; it is on those documents they believe the validity of testing hangs. And because of their significance, most testing programs (whether local, state, or national) incorporate experts in the field of education to write them. For the NAEP tests, teachers and professors from around the country descend on Princeton to create the rubrics used to score the items. For state and local tests, usually state and local teachers are hired to undertake the task. It is believed the participation of those educators—the sharing of their wisdom and experience from a lifetime in the classroom—is what really gives those rubrics their significance, their power.

Meanwhile, as those education experts argue interminably about whether a top-level response should be called "complete" or "comprehensive," those of us who actually use the rubrics to assess student responses sit idly by, a bit bored with a debate we know has almost nothing to do with our jobs. While it might be testing sacrilege to say so, we know there's virtually no difference between "complete" and "comprehensive," at least not to the people paid to score the tests. We know those rubrics aren't the most important part of test scoring, not at all—they are no more than a jumping-off point to begin the process. In fact, in recent years I'd taken to replacing the rubrics and substituted for them what I was calling "scoring charts." I wasn't doing it to try to make a grab for power or to undermine the entire history of standardized test scoring, and honestly, it was a bit bothersome and time-consuming to have to make those charts. That said, I *had* to do it, because my scorers were beginning to seem ever less capable of actually understanding the rubrics provided.

For instance, in the spring of 2006, I trained a group of scorers to assess student responses written to questions about E. B. White's *Charlotte's Web*. The final question asked the students for an opinion about White's work *and* support from the text. It read:

> In *Charlotte's Web*, does Charlotte prove to be a good friend to the pig Wilbur? Support your position with at least two examples from the text.

The rubric, including examples of student responses, looked like the one on page 191.

Frankly, the rubric was perfectly clear. Anyone who could read should have been able to implement the decisions it outlined. They *should* have. Still, my scorers struggled. Not all of them, of course, but more than a couple.

2006 Reading

Charlotte's Web

4 The response shows complete understanding of the question by providing a relevant opinion and two examples from the text in support of that opinion.

I do think Charlotte was a good friend because she talked to Wilbur when he was lonely and she saved him with her message in the web.

3 The response shows partial understanding of the question by providing either a relevant opinion AND one example from the text in support OR two examples from the text in support of an unstated opinion.

Charlotte was a good friend becuz when she spun her message in her web then Wilbur wouldn't die.

There was the time she first talked to him and the time she wrote the words.

2 The response shows minimal understanding of the question by providing either a relevant opinion about Charlotte's friendship OR an example from the text in support of an unstated opinion.

I think it's obvious she was an excellent friend.

When she first talked to him in his stall when he was very lonely.

1 The response shows no understanding of the question by providing neither a relevant opinion about Charlotte's friendship NOR any examples from the text of that friendship.

No/Yes

She died at the end of the story.

Templeton is a rat.

After the group had looked at the Anchor Papers, we started to review the practice set. "Darlene, please read and score #1," I said. "And tell me what you gave it." Darlene read the response aloud:

> In *Charlotte's Web,* does Charlotte prove to be a good friend to the pig Wilbur? Support your position with at least two examples from the test.
> *Of course she was a good friend to Wilbur. Her message in the web saved his life.*

"OK," Darlene said. "I'm giving it a 2."

"Why a 2?"

"Well, it has either a position *or* support, like the rubric says for 2."

I looked at the rubric. "It only has one of those things, not both?"

"No," she said. "It has both a position and support. That's why it's getting a 2."

"But position *and* support gets a 3," I said. "Right?"

She stared at the rubric. "Well, it has enough for a 2, position *or* support. Plus, it seems to have enough for a 3, position *and* support. So what should I do?"

Because I'd been down that road many times before, I knew exactly what Darlene should do. She should use my handy scoring chart, a rubric of sorts but in diagram form. "Use this," I said to Darlene, handing out my scoring chart to the whole team (see page 193).

"Look," I said. "There's only one way to get a 4, right? Two different ways to get a 3, two different ways to get a 2, and only one way to get a 1. Read the response and find out where on the chart it fits, *capiche*?"

Those people who had some sense and already understood the original rubric nodded. Those people like Darlene who

2005 Reading

Charlotte's Web

4 RELEVANT   EXAMPLE FROM   EXAMPLE FROM
   OPINION   +   TEXT   +   TEXT

3 RELEVANT OPINION   EXAMPLE FROM TEXT
   +   +
   EXAMPLE FROM TEXT   EXAMPLE FROM TEXT

2 RELEVANT OPINION   EXAMPLE FROM
   ONLY   TEXT **ONLY**

1 NO RELEVANT OPINION
   +
   NO EXAMPLE FROM TEXT

hadn't mastered the original rubric looked at my scoring chart, and the lightbulbs flashed.

"Aha!" Darlene said. "So #1 has an opinion and one example from the test, so it *has* to be a 3, right?"

"Correct," I said.

"Well, damn," Darlene complained. "Why didn't you hand us out this chart to begin with?"

I hadn't handed out the chart because I knew how hallowed that original rubric was supposed to be. I hadn't handed out the chart originally because I knew by doing so I was proving all those many words on the rubrics the teacher/writers bickered constantly about (Was the understanding "complete" or "partial"? Was the position "pertinent"?) were virtually irrelevant. Handing out scoring charts meant those wordy rubrics weren't the sacred scrolls everyone imagined, and no one in the business was ready yet to make that claim.

I had come to believe rubrics *weren't* the sacred scrolls of standardized test scoring only after years of experience, because by the spring of 2006 I had seen them go awry for nearly 15 years, for myriad reasons. Some rubrics failed as assessors of "standardized" test scoring because they were theoretically unsound, but most went to hell simply because they were open to so many interpretations *and* because there were so many student responses to score. A rubric that might work great with one teacher and 20 students often ended up like a Laurel and Hardy routine by the time it was being used by 20 scorers to assess 100,000 student responses.

One of the first questions I worked on, in 1994 back in that stinky underground basement of the abandoned Iowa City shopping mall, asked the students to identify the protagonists in a story called "The Lion and the Squirrel." Basically the story was a knock-off of Aesop's story of "The Lion and the Mouse"—when the Lion catches the Mouse but lets him live, and days later the Mouse returns the favor by helping the Lion escape a hunter's snare—and in replying to the question, many of the students confused the "Lion and the Squirrel" story they had read with the "Lion and the Mouse" story with which they were well acquainted. As a result, many student responses talked about the "mouse" as a lead character when they probably meant the "squirrel." Because that didn't really indicate any misunderstanding of the story's theme (the weak or small can help the strong and big), the decision was made by my supervisor to credit the answer "mouse" as well as "squirrel." It seemed fair at the time, and no one in my group disagreed with the decision—basically we opted to cut those kids a break.

As the responses poured in by the thousands, however, that meant in no time we were crediting responses that said "squirrel" as well as those saying "sqrle" or "sguirl" or "skerril." We were also crediting "mouse" or "mice" or "moose," even though there wasn't any mouse in the actual story on the test. Eventually we were also crediting "rat" and "ratse" (c'mon, how different is that from a mouse to a 10-year-old?), even though you couldn't find that pest in either "The Lion and the Squirrel" *or* "The Lion and the Mouse." And finally, we ended up accepting, well, "any rodent," because what were both squirrels and mice (and rats and beavers), except "nibbling mammals of the order Rodentia."

In other words, if a student said one of the protagonists of "The Lion and the Squirrel" was a lemming, a shrew, or a hamster (all rodents, which we knew after my supervisor's visit to the Iowa City Public Library), that answer was on the way to earning full credit. All the student had to do to get maximum points for that response was to also identify the other lead character as a "lion," and by "lion," naturally, I mean "lion" or "tiger" or "leopard" or "panther" or "bobcat" . . . .

So while we credited "lion and squirrel" as the protagonists, we also accepted "lion and mouse," "big cat and mouse," "tiger and mouse," "tiger and rat," "leopard and rat," "leopard and hamster," "panther and hamster," "bobcat and hamster," "bobcat and shrew," and on and on. Fortunately, there were more of the former answers than the latter, but still, what can I say? It seemed fair at the time.

Particularly interesting about that experience is that I was involved in scoring the same item again the next year, with a different supervisor, and the second supervisor was aghast at what had previously occurred. "What's all this crap about rodents?" she demanded. Not getting a satisfactory answer, my new supervisor completely overruled the scoring decisions made the year before, and she decided credit would be given as protagonists only to the responses "lion" and "squirrel." Not only was "mouse" not going to be given credit, neither was "tiger" or "rat" or "bobcat" or "beaver."

"Ridiculous," she said of the last year's work.

The rubric, it should be understood, never changed. The first year it said full credit would be awarded to student responses "for correctly identifying the story's two protagonists," and the next year it said exactly the same thing. Of course it did, because that was one of the sacrosanct tenets of the standardized testing industry: the rubric would *never* change. It was inviolable, written and approved by schoolteachers. In the case of the Lion and Squirrel/Tiger and Beaver, the only thing that changed was how the rubric was used, so a student response earning full credit the first year for identifying the story's lead characters as a "tiger and a mouse" would earn exactly no credit the second year for that very same answer, not so much as a single point.

It happened all the time. A trainer would make some reasonable interpretation of how to use a rubric and would get approval on how to score the student responses from a range-finding committee, and the next year a new trainer would make a different reasonable interpretation of the rubric and override the previous decisions he or she didn't like. One time I saw a science trainer decide *not* to accept the answer "recycling" as a way to reduce carbon dioxide in the atmosphere (because she said so much energy was used in the recycling process), but the next year a new trainer opted to go ahead and *credit* "recycling" as an acceptable response. That change in scoring was never officially recorded anywhere, and hence statistical comparisons of the two years' students were still made, even if the same answer got different scores in different years.

Most problems occurred simply because there were so many student responses. The differences between the tens of thousands of answers would be miniscule, and if you followed a seemingly logical trail when doling out points, you'd often end up in bizarre places on the rubric. Once I trained a science item on decomposers (the organisms in the ocean, like bacteria and fungi, that break down the final remains of living things), with the question asking students to identify their purpose. The real purpose of the decomposers is to recycle minerals and nutrients back into the marine food chain, but if you kept accepting answers that were *close* to that ("they provide food," "they deliver food," "they make food"), soon enough you ended up crediting the idea of decomposers "serving food to the other fish." Who knows how it happened, but a couple of days into the project and there I was accepting the idea of decomposers "serving food to the other fish," not recycling minerals and nutrients at all but a bunch of tiny waiters delivering seafood platters to their cohorts down at the bottom of the sea.

Another time I trained an item on biomagnification (the process in which toxic substances in living things *increase* as they go up the food chain), and I was stunned at the end of scoring to discover my group had been giving partial credit to answers saying "pollutants *diminish* in power as they go up the food chain." That answer was the antithesis of biomagnification— the *exact opposite* of what it is!—yet somehow I'd instructed my team to give partial credit to responses like that. I didn't know how I ended up making that decision, but amid the waves of thousands and thousands of student responses, I *did* make it. At some point that response must have seemed no worse to me than some other ambiguous response I'd been giving partial credit to, and the next thing I knew my group was giving points to an answer that theoretically could not have been more wrong.

Once I saw a trainer instruct his scorers to give full credit to the idea a wildlife expert was "observing," "watching," "following," or "tracking" a herd of elephants but only partial credit to the idea he was "studying" them. How he made that distinction I'll never know. I saw another trainer telling her scorers to give the answer "I don't know" partial credit for one item, because she thought "I don't know" was a not unreasonable reply to a question about predicting the weather. For more than a decade I'd seen student responses of "I don't know" always get the same score—zero points—but one day on a whim that trainer changed everything and decided it was worth at least something. She consulted no one, recorded this monumental decision nowhere, just blithely made up her mind and went with it. She thought "I don't know" had become worthy of points, at least for that item on that day.

Her actions summed up my world of test scoring perfectly. The decision to credit "I don't know" seemed right to her at the time, so she credited it, which was an impetuousness I understood completely. I acted the same way myself. I would make some judgment about how to interpret a rubric and be completely comfortable with that, and then reading a hundred more student responses, I'd cancel my earlier scoring edict and replace it with another. My scorers would be crossing out on their rubrics something I'd told them a half hour before, replacing it with something else I was then convinced was infallible, immutable, utter genius. I might not have believed that in another hour, but right then I sure did.

That was my abiding experience in the world of standardized test scoring: things change, rules change, scores change. Because of that reality—because of the endless uncertainty we often faced—my favorite rubric of all time is the joke rubric posted on the office wall of a friend of mine:

The Real Rubric

10 This response shows evidence of Pretty Darned Close to Visionary Comprehension.

9 This response shows evidence of Rich But Not Quite Extraordinary Comprehension.

8 This response shows evidence of Rock Solid Comprehension.

7   This response shows evidence of On the Right Track Comprehension.

6   This response shows evidence of Not Completely Useless Comprehension.

5   This response shows evidence of Nothing to Sneeze At Comprehension.

4   This response shows evidence of Getting There Comprehension.

3   This response shows evidence of Not Too, Too Bad Comprehension.

2   This response shows evidence of Some Brain Activity Comprehension.

1   This response shows evidence of Not Even a Blip of Comprehension.

The first time I saw that rubric, I laughed aloud. Everyone who works in testing does. We don't laugh because the rubric is so funny, however, just because it's true. We laugh because we know that at its heart the work we do is indefinable, no more than the gut-level lumping of student responses into random piles of various permutations of "good" and "not so good," an ambiguity that is undeniable and is summed up perfectly by "The Real Rubric" hanging on my friend's office wall. We also laugh because we know, unfortunately, that there's no other sacred rubric—not even one written by the saintliest of schoolteachers or the most esteemed of professors—that can change one simple fact about the scoring of open-ended questions on standardized tests: the best of rubrics are always just trumped by the deluge of student responses they are written to assess.

Warm Bodies

THE ONLY REASON I accepted another job scoring tests in the spring of 2007 is because I was made an offer I couldn't refuse. At the time, I was happily ensconced in the East Village of New York City, trying to make it as a writer: I'd already gotten a couple of magazine stories published, and I never would have returned to testing except an ex-colleague of mine wanted to ship me to Iowa City for three weeks to train the scoring of the NAEP reading test. As that sounded like nothing to me but a paid vacation to my beloved former Shangri-La, I stopped writing long enough to undertake the task.

The fun began for me for NAEP reading 2007 even before I left my apartment, when I sat through yet another ridiculous conference call, this one barely audible due to a bad phone connection. On the line were more than 30 people, including me in New York and representatives of ETS, Pearson Education, various federal government agencies, and the NAEP Reading Committee spread all over the United States. We were all looking at copies of student responses that had been FedEx'ed to us. We were in the preliminary stages of deciding how to score the papers when a contentious debate broke out over a single student response. I wasn't paying very close attention to yet another testy exchange about a single response when something began to dawn on me: the argument I was barely listening to didn't even seem to be about the student's *score*; it simply seemed to be about which paper we were supposed to be looking at. Because the phone connection for the conference call was so poor, our huge group couldn't even get that straight:

Disembodied Voice: Did you say we're on Paper 3E right now?

Different Disembodied Voice: 3E? No. We're on 3D.

Yet Another Disembodied Voice: CD?

Angry Disembodied Voice: Look, we're on Paper 3D right now. Three! D!

Different Disembodied Voice: BC?

Discrete Random Disembodied Voice: The response that says "my heartfelt opinion"?

Angry Disembodied Voice: We are on Paper 3D! One . . . 2 . . . 3!!!! A . . . B . . . C . . . D!!!

{Silence}

Disembodied Voice: Regardless of what paper we're on, are we assessing the understanding of persuasive text here or story elements? What am I really looking for?

Different Disembodied Voice: What are you looking for? That seems like something you should know.

Yet Another Disembodied Voice: Well, the bigger problem is I don't think I like the question anymore.

Random Disembodied Voice: . . . late for that . . . .

Disembodied Voice: What was that? Did someone say something?

Angry Disembodied Voice: Let's start again, OK? Everyone back to the first paper. The one that says . . . A . . . 1 . . . on the top right corner and has the number 78 on the bottom of the page. Everyone got that?

{Silence}

Angry Disembodied Voice: OK, so what score are we giving this?

Different Disembodied Voice: I gave it a 3. A low 3, but a 3.

Random Disembodied Voice: I'd say a high 2.

Different Disembodied Voice: Better than some other 2's but not a 3 in my book.

Random Different Disembodied Voice: Seems more 4-like, to me but I'll concede and go along with the will of the group.

Angry Disembodied Voice: Hallelujah.

Different Disembodied Voice: So what exactly are we arguing here?

Random Disembodied Voice: I wouldn't say it's a 3, but I didn't really understand the examples on the rubrics, either, so . . . .

Random Different Disembodied Voice: . . . but . . . less important . . . .

Angry Disembodied Voice: OK, so what score are we giving this?

Different Angry Disembodied Voice: OK, let's try again. How about if we look at a paper that we can agree on? Let's look at A3.

Random Disembodied Voice: AC?

Angry Disembodied Voice: *A! Three!* This paper is clearly a 4. We can at least agree on that, right? Clearly a 4?

[At first there is silence, but then laughter. The laughter is random to begin with, but soon it is heard filling the scratchy phone lines. Everyone is laughing, because the 30-odd people who have found Paper A3 have all discovered the same thing: Although it was said to be "clearly a 4," on the top of

the student response the dark black number of "3" has been crossed out and replaced with a thin, penciled-in "4." The response that was "clearly a 4" had obviously once been scored a 3.]

> *Angry Disembodied Voice, Now Disheartened*: Oh, well, ...

Things didn't get a lot better when I got to Princeton, when the ETS staff met face to face with the NAEP Reading Committee to make the final decisions about the scoring of that year's items. Although fewer people were involved in the discussions at that point, and although we were no longer hampered by a poor phone connection, that meeting wasn't exactly the epitome of standardization itself. In deciding how to score the single question we'd spent the entire morning debating, the first day of the meeting concluded as such:

> *Expert Educator/Committee Member*: Back to the polar bear question. What did we say the score for Paper A1 was, a 3 or a 2?
>
> *Different Expert Educator/Committee Member*: We said a 2.
>
> *ETS Staffer*: No, we said 3.
>
> *Third Expert Educator/Committee Member*: Yeah, it has to be a 3 because it's better than A4, which is a 2.
>
> *Second ETS Staffer*: Who said A4 was a 2?
>
> *Fourth Expert Educator/Committee Member*: I thought this was a two-point scale? How's anyone getting a 3?
>
> *Third ETS Staffer*: Yes, I do think we decided to go with a two-point scale.
>
> *Expert Educator/Committee Member*: Well, if it's a two-point scale, then we have a whole bunch of other issues . . . .
>
> {Silence}
>
> *ETS Staffer*: A1 is a what?
>
> {Silence}

Second Expert Educator/Committee Member: Speaking of other issues, I think it might be time to tweak this item again. I'm not sure it's getting at what we want cognitively.

ETS Project Manager, clapping her hands together: Oh, goodie! I love this part of the meeting.

Random Expert Educator/Committee Member, sounding unsure: What part of the meeting is that?

ETS Project Manager: You know, the part of the meeting when you, the committee, complain about the items written by you, the committee . . . .

{Silence. Nervous laughter}

Expert Educator/Committee Member: So where are we going to dinner tonight, anyway?

{End of Scene}

The scoring of the 2007 NAEP reading project didn't go to hell for my team until about three hours into the first day, but that was actually no more than 30 minutes after I'd first met my team of scorers. I'd spent the first couple of hours of the day knocking around the Pearson/Iowa City scoring center, familiarizing myself with the building where last I'd worked on 2000 NAEP science while also getting reacquainted with some of my old friends from my NCS days. My team of scorers, meanwhile, was sitting through its lengthy HR orientation, but by about 10 A.M. they had at last reported to our cubicle to begin work. When they finally got there, I introduced myself and Heidi, the Pearson scoring supervisor who would assist me, and then I asked the scorers to tell me their names and a little bit about themselves.

In the front row sat Dale, a first-time scorer who looked like he was going to pass out from his fear of public speaking. Next to him was Michi, who stumbled over the English language but who cheerfully told us she was very thankful for the job at Pearson because she'd recently been fired from another test-scoring gig at neighboring ACT. Beside Michi sat a tiny, terrified old woman who said only that her name was Alice. In the second row were Abdullah and Henry, the former an aspiring graduate student and the latter a military retiree. Beside them was Bill, a distinguished-looking elderly fellow, and Nate, a curly-haired youngster who was beginning law school at the University of Iowa the next fall. In the back row sat two 40-something women already deeply immersed in what would turn out to be a three-week gabfest. The blonde was Mary, who didn't exactly endear herself to the other members of the team by announcing that she had forgone her lucrative law career because she felt like "a change," a declaration that clearly puzzled those scorers who had no employment options other than their current, temporary, 10-buck-an-hour scoring job. The brunette was Betty, and although at first she had to be coaxed into talking about herself, she ultimately wouldn't shut up, her lengthy introduction eventually including both most of her life story and a couple of exhaustive lists of Betty's likes (organic foods, free-range farming, natural incense) and dislikes (the war in Iraq, George W. Bush, standardized testing).

I laughed hearing the last one. "You don't like standardized testing?" I teased. "So what are you doing here?"

Betty didn't smile even a bit. "I'm diabetic," she replied. "Have to pay for my insulin somehow."

Having established everyone's motives for being at the Pearson site that morning (Mary as something of a lark, the other scorers because they needed money, and me for a free trip to Iowa City), it was time to start determining the state of reading comprehension of America's students. To begin I had the group read the first passage aloud, having the scorers each read one or two paragraphs of the story of Dallas, a youngster who moved from Illinois to Florida and became the first girl to play on her new school's football team. Having my teams read aloud was something I always did, because it allowed me to glean some understanding of each scorer's facility with the English language. Having *that* team read aloud also meant I could hear—even before we'd finished the story—that we were doomed: "facility with the English language" wasn't a quality you would attribute to many members of that group.

Bill read first, and while he was a retired banker, he was also an aged fellow with thick glasses, a guy who read slowly, painfully slowly, his voice quavering throughout as he traced the words on the page with his shaking forefinger. Dale went next, quietly, oh-so-quietly, his voice completely without emotion or inflection whether he was reading something happy, sad, or indifferent. At the moment in the story when the girl celebrated an exciting victory with the single exuberant cry "Yes!" Dale read the word as if he were the computer-generated voice of an ATM: "yes." Later he read the sentence "She was sad" in an identical flat tone, and I can't say I was surprised when weeks after he read a beautiful sentence from a Mark Twain story ("a single leafy bough that glowed like a flame in the unobstructed splendor that was flowing from the sun") in that same moribund monotone. Regardless of the circumstances of the story or the language used to convey it, Dale articulated no difference at all.

Michi followed, and while she read her excerpt more eloquently than I could read anything in a language other than English, she also read it as someone speaking a second language, stumbling over simple words and mispronouncing others, completely confusing verb tenses and skipping articles. Henry read next, correctly but methodically, a retired military man making sure to dot the *i*'s and cross the *t*'s without necessarily showing any appreciation for the prose. Both Betty and Mary read functionally, and I was thrilled to hear young Nate orate like Cicero, with eloquence and strength. Abdullah didn't have as difficult a time as Michi did, but he, too, suffered from reading in his second language; while Alice, the dear, old woman hunched fearfully in the corner of the front row, read her excerpt slowly and quietly, her fingers also tracing the words on the page, all of us leaning forward to hear her tiny, tinny voice.

When the group was done, I wondered if the fourth graders taking the assessment had read the story any better. Although we were about to begin scoring student responses on a *reading* test, I actually doubted the abilities of some of my team to even perform that task: Michi and Abdullah's renditions indicated trouble comprehending the words, and while Bill's and Alice's readings were correct, I questioned whether either could remember the language they had uttered aloud. As for both Dale and Henry, I didn't doubt they could read, only that they could understand. I think both saw words on paper, not anything those words might represent. While I was relatively confident in the abilities of the others to read (Betty, Mary, and Nate), that still left me with questions about the comprehension skills of two-thirds of the team.

Given the motley crew of scorers working under me, it wasn't too surprising when the scoring of that project tanked almost immediately, with the reliability numbers plummeting dangerously low. The numbers dropped because of all the usual reasons (ambiguous rubrics, impending deadlines, a ceaseless flood of student responses), but the biggest problem was the scorers themselves. I don't say that to be unkind, and in fact I spent a very pleasant three weeks working with those people. Even if we had occasional spats during our training discussions, for the most part the dynamic between the nine scorers, Heidi, and me was one of cooperative goodwill. Conceding, however, that my team was a fine group of decent people, that still didn't mean I'd want them deciding *my* fate. Allowing that team to make important decisions about anyone's future didn't seem like too good an idea to me, and you can bet I'd have raised a considerable stink if I'd known my life would be affected by any choices made by that group, especially Michi. Michi was nearly 60 years old and had moved to Iowa City from Japan to live with her doctor-daughter, but she said as much as she loved this country, she was having a hard time finding work.

"ACT fire me," she said. "I like Pearson because they no fire me." Every time Michi said it, she would smile wide, her pride at being loyal to the company abundantly clear.

Michi did love the job. Every time we trained a new item, she would giggle about what a good time we were having. "Funny," Michi would say to me, "you funny," a compliment I didn't take too much to heart as I was pretty sure she didn't even understand most of my sly asides. Still, so many things made her explode with glee, like when one student described as "cute" how Dallas felt about being named an honorary team captain for one game.

"Cute!" Michi roared, laughing and laughing. "She feel 'cute.'"

As funny as Michi found the answer, she was shocked when told it would get credit. "Cute?" Michi asked. "Cute is feeling? No."

"Yes," Heidi and I told her. "You should definitely credit 'She thought it was a cute move.'"

"No," Michi said, shaking her head in disbelief. "No . . . ."

Yes, we told her, yes, but it was that lack of understanding of the English language that hindered Michi most on the project. She had a hard time recognizing examples of both American vernacular and more sophisticated vocabulary words. Once Heidi was backreading Michi's scores, and she called me over to show me a response that Michi had given the lowest possible score to, a 1 on a three-point scale. The question had asked how Dallas felt seeing her aunt dancing wildly in the bleachers when the young girl had first taken the field, and the students were supposed to be credited for any answer reflecting Dallas's negative feelings about her aunt's excitability in the stands. The rubric listed examples of acceptable responses like "Dallas didn't like it," "She frowned," or "Dallas was ashamed."

But the response on which Michi had given the score of 1 didn't say "She frowned" or "She didn't like it." The response on which Michi had given the score of 1 was "Dallas found her aunt's behavior irksome and disappointing. She was embarrassed by the dancing, which she mentioned negatively."

It was the single best answer I'd seen in the entire time we scored that question, yet Michi had given the lowest possible score. The fact the answer was written by a fourth grader was amazing, but the fact Michi hadn't given it even *partial* credit was nearly incomprehensible. Still, when Heidi and I showed the response to Michi to tell her to credit responses like that, our scorer remained unconvinced.

"'Irksome' not on rubric," Michi said. "What is embasser . . . embrass . . . ?"

"Embarrassed," I said. "Embarrassed is nearly a perfect answer."

"Not on rubric," Michi said.

"Put on rubric," I told her.

"OK," she smiled, but it didn't help. There were always new words popping up in the student responses Michi had never seen before ("frustrated," "disturbed"), and she would regularly fail to credit those answers because she didn't know them.

Language wasn't Michi's only problem, though, and she also managed to misscore papers our team had scored as a group and papers that matched exactly the examples given on the rubric. Michi basically misscored a considerable number of the responses that showed up on the computer screen in front of her, but Heidi and I decided to ignore that fact because Michi was such a joy to be around. Her constant giggling and infectious laugh made Michi very popular in our cubicle—she made a sometimes unbearable job a bit more bearable—so

Heidi and I figured we'd keep the sweetheart employed even if she was doing an atrocious job. The only other option, of course, was to get Michi fired, and that was an unpleasantness neither Heidi nor I (temporary employees ourselves) wanted any part of.

Michi wasn't the only one screwing up, however—not even close. Abdullah wasn't a great scorer himself, for some of the same reasons as Michi and for other reasons that were his problem alone. First, Abdullah's scoring also suffered because English wasn't his native tongue, and he was often stumped by both complex words and simple idioms. He misscored one student response because he didn't know *mortified* meant much the same thing as *embarrassed*, while he erred in scoring others because he didn't know *bummed out* meant "depressed," *grossed out* meant "disgusted," or that "Dallas was feeling him" meant the young girl was actually fond of the team's star quarterback, not that she was literally touching him. Abdullah misscored another response because he didn't know Dallas saying football "completed her" was another way of saying she "liked it," which he'd have known only if he'd seen the classic tearjerker movie *Jerry Maguire*.

Abdullah's other problem was that his background was in science and we were working on a reading test, and his lack of familiarity with certain literary terms seriously hampered his ability to assess student responses. A couple of weeks into the project we were scoring 12th-grade tests, and whenever I mentioned different types of figurative language, Abdullah would immediately thrust his hand in the air to pepper me with questions.

"Excuse me, sir," he would say. "What is this 'alliteration'?"

What is this personification, he asked? This simile? This metaphor? Because Abdullah sincerely wanted to know, I did attempt to explain each to him, and although Abdullah copied my definitions down word for word, he didn't exactly become an expert on figurative language based only on my 30-second explanations of it. For the most part, Abdullah still didn't understand, but he didn't let that slow him down and continued to do his darnedest while scoring those tests. Sure, he may have misscored a significant number of the student responses, but I couldn't really blame him: as it had been hard to fault the charming Michi for her inability to correctly score tests written in a language other than Japanese, it was equally hard to fault the earnest Abdullah for not having a comprehensive knowledge of English figurative language given his engineering degree had been earned at a Yemeni university where the classes were taught in Arabic.

A number of the native English speakers had troubles themselves. Bill might not have been the worst scorer, but he was certainly the slowest. He sat at a computer in the middle row, in front of the computers that Heidi and I used in the back, and the two of us would often watch the elderly Bill as he scored the student responses. While most of the answers were only a sentence or two long, and while most of the scorers would get through about 150 of them an hour, Bill spent minutes on each response, not because he was being so particular but because he was being so slow. Once I looked up to see an answer on his screen, and then after I'd been around the cubicle to deal with some questions, I returned to my desk to see the same response still in front of Bill. I could see from the back row that the response said "Dallas liked it," which was an example given on the rubric for the score point 2, yet Bill continued to stare at the answer on his screen although there was no question how many points the response deserved.

"Are you seeing this?" I whispered to Heidi.

"Yeah," she nodded. "About five minutes that one's been up there."

For another five minutes Bill kept trying to score that single response. He squinted at the answer on his screen; he squinted at the training papers as he sloooowly paged through his notebook; he squinted at his rubric, moving it closer and farther away from his face while pointing his index finger at the words on the page. Heidi and I had stopped doing our own work entirely and were instead watching Bill, who at some point raised his hand. I thought that scoring drama might come to an end when Heidi or I went up to answer his question, but Bill dropped his hand even before either of us could get out of our chairs. Instead of asking for help, Bill went back to squinting and thinking, looking from the student response to the rubric to the training papers again and again.

A good five minutes after I'd returned to my desk to find that same answer still on his screen, Bill put down his rubric and finally reached his trembling right hand over toward his computer mouse. Bill maneuvered the mouse to move the cursor on the screen over toward the three scoring buttons situated at the bottom of the page: the 1, 2, and 3 buttons. As Heidi and I leaned forward together in eager anticipation, Bill dragged the cursor from the 3 button ("No!" she whispered), to the 2 button ("Oh, God, yes," I mumbled), to the 1 button ("Aaahh," we both said), before he circled back and left the cursor directly atop the 2. Because Bill's hand was shaking slightly, the cursor on the screen was shaking slightly, too, but at least it had stopped directly over the very button Heidi and I were so desperate for Bill to click. To our absolute delight, Bill then mustered up his courage and his strength and pressed down his finger, finally registering for that student response the appropriate score of 2.

"Hallelujah!" Heidi whispered. "He did it!"

The job shouldn't have been that hard, and even if test scoring often included dealing with aberrant answers or ambiguous delineations between score points, many student responses still should have been simple to score. A large percentage of the student responses that showed up on the computer screens were similar to the training papers or comparable to the examples given on the rubric, and the job really was no more than a big matching game: If a response looked like Anchor Paper #1, you gave it a 3, and if it looked like Anchor Paper #9, you gave it a 1. If a rubric said "she liked it" earned a 2, then when a response showed up that said "she dug it," you gave that a 2, also. It wasn't very complex work, but while neither Heidi nor I had any difficulty doing it, most of the scorers on our team did. The job, in fact, was really only mastered by two of the nine scorers in our group, the retiring attorney, Mary, and the aspiring attorney, Nate.

While Mary was a consistent and accurate scorer, young Nate proved to be so invaluable I took to calling him the Boy Genius. Not only did the Boy Genius score the student responses correctly (remembering our training, making good decisions, matching papers to the right anchors, recognizing responses we had talked about as a group), he also scored them at break-neck speed. While many of Nate's teammates were unsure of themselves and couldn't click the scoring button without hectoring me or Heidi with questions, Nate just scored and scored.

At the end of every day, Nate checked the total number of responses scored, because he wanted to know how many tests he'd scored compared to the other members of the team. Nate had reason to be proud, because every single day the Boy Genius scored at least *twice* as many student responses as did everyone else on the team, and some days he actually scored more than the rest of the team *combined*. Given the other scorers were going so slowly, and given they were also incorrectly scoring way too many responses, it was largely the work of the Boy Genius that even allowed us to finish the project at all. The only problem Nate faced doing the job was one of motivation, as it wasn't exactly challenging work. Only once did his frustration get the best of him, though, the day the Boy Genius slammed his hands down on the desk and rolled his chair away from his computer, dropping his head into his hands and wailing, "It's so booooring!"

Nate's teammates, in contrast, weren't really bored; they were mostly baffled. In the back row, the aging hippy Betty showed up each day in sandals and tie-dyed T-shirts, and while she managed to be perfectly passionate and articulate about any number of topical issues (Why was marijuana illegal? What was happening to the Iowa family farm? Who had actually voted for George W. Bush?), she frequently failed to understand the simplest of scoring rules.

"Saying the story is about 'animals' is considered vague and only gets a 2," I told her one day. "Saying it's about 'African parrots' is specific and gets a 3."

"I don't see the difference," she said.

"'Animals' is a generality," I said, "but 'African parrots' is directly out of the passage, here on the third paragraph of the second page, right?" Although I was pointing out to her the example in the story, Betty wasn't buying it.

"I still don't see the difference," she told me.

"You disagree with the rule, or you actually cannot differentiate between those two responses?" I asked.

"I'm not sure," she said. "I'm only sure I don't know what I'm supposed to be doing."

Another time she asked, "How is 'because she went to a new team' any different from 'because she went to a new football team'?"

"The difference is the word *football*," I smiled.

"And that matters?" Betty asked.

"It does in the training papers, so I guess so."

"I don't get it," she muttered again.

The one scorer in my group who actually got me thinking about having someone fired was Alice, the little old lady who sat silently in the corner of the front row. Alice was about five feet tall and 100 pounds, with a head full of white hair. During the introductions, she had told us no more than her first name, and for the rest of the project, she said little more than that. She simply sat in the corner, silently assessing student responses, but even her willingness to work hard wasn't that helpful: Alice was putting the wrong scores on the student responses so regularly I realized at some point she might even be challenging Michi for the title of Worst Scorer Ever.

Before my team had shown up on the first morning of the project, Heidi had said how lucky we were to get Alice. Alice was very "experienced," Heidi told me, and while I had foolishly interpreted that to mean she was "expert" or "qualified," it seemed in Pearson corporate-speak "experienced" really meant only that she'd been working that dead-end, part-time, low-paying scoring job for a hell of a long time. As "experienced" as Alice might have been, however, the very real fact was that she seemed to have almost no idea what she was doing. During one training session, I saw her "reading" from a rubric that she held completely upside down, and when during another I asked her to read Anchor Paper #10, Alice instead started reading *Practice* Paper #10. Although for the last hour the group had been reading and discussing the Anchor Papers, Alice had held in front of her and pretended to understand a completely different set of student responses.

Given her inability to follow the training, it wasn't too surprising to discover that Alice's scoring was all over the place. She was giving 1's to responses that deserved 3's, and 3's to responses that deserved 1's, and also every other incorrect score in between (3's to 2's, 2's to 1's, 1's to 2's, etc.). While at first I thought Alice's wildly inappropriate scoring was just silly, at some point I began to get perturbed.

"What's going on here, Heidi?" I asked the supervisor who had told me how lucky we were to get Alice. "We can't let her keep scoring wrong forever, can we?"

"She'll get better," promised Heidi, who then made a point of giving Alice an extra half hour of training. That extra tutoring didn't help, unfortunately, and by the time we started scoring a four-point item Alice had taken her mis-scoring to a whole new level of incompetence.

The four-point question had asked the students to describe the temperament of the football player Dallas, with points being awarded for text-based descriptions of the girl's character plus appropriate examples from the story in support. Alice, predictably, didn't understand, and the first response of hers I backread I saw that she had given the highest possible score to a response that was no more than a story summary. The response made absolutely no mention of any of the character traits we were supposed to credit for Dallas (that she was "optimistic," "hardworking," etc.), instead rambling on with plot details. There was absolutely no question the answer deserved a 1—it looked exactly like a couple of the training papers given 1's— yet Alice had scored it slightly differently: she had given the response a 4.

By giving the highest level score to a response that deserved the least possible points, Alice had erred as much as theoretically possible. Her score of 4 indicated absolutely no understanding of how we were supposed to be scoring. Although Alice had already sat through both our complete training session and an additional half-hour review with Heidi, I decided to print out a copy of that student response to discuss it with her myself.

"Excuse me, Alice," I said gently, kneeling beside her. "I need to talk to you about this one student response."

She answered without making eye contact. "OK," she said.

"You've given this paper a 4, but it never talks about Dallas's temperament. It just talks about the story's plot."

Alice still wasn't looking at me. "OK," she said.

"Remember," I continued, "we give points for correct examples of her temperament, like 'hardworking' or 'brave,' not just what happened in the story."

Alice nodded. "OK," she said.

I didn't want to be patronizing, but I also didn't know if Alice was actually following me. "So no points for plot details," I reiterated, "but points for temperament or character traits, right?"

"OK," she said, repeating the only word she said during my entire visit. I might've wanted to say more to Alice, might've wanted to ask her questions to see if she actually knew what I was talking about, but I felt so bad for the seemingly terrified woman I decided to just end my "training" session with her right there. Walking back to my desk, I might've liked to think all of Alice's "OKs" indicated some epiphany on her part, but I knew very well the best interpretation of that repeated utterance was something else indeed. It was pretty clear every time Alice said "OK" to me, what she really meant was "Please go away."

My tutoring session with Alice had exactly as much effect as Heidi's earlier efforts, and I realized an hour later I'd wasted my time when I backread another of the answers Alice had scored. I knew she had misscored that response as soon as I'd read the first three words.

"Confident and determined," the response began. "Dallas is confident because she believes she can make the team even when the coach tells her he's never had a girl player, and determined because she wins the big game by scoring a touchdown even when the big boy is trying to tackle her."

It was a nearly perfect answer: The response deserved a 2 after those first three words (for providing two accurate, text-based characteristics of Dallas), and it deserved a 4 by the end. Alice, however, had given the response a 1, assessing as the lowest possible score an answer deserving the most possible credit, her score completely confirming her total lack of understanding of what we were doing.

When I showed the response to Heidi, at first she frowned but then just shrugged. "Oh, let her go," Heidi smiled. "After all, we've got the pull button."

Ah, the magical pull button, that magnificent tool helping Heidi and me perpetrate a massive reliability cover-up. Heidi was a woman I knew from NCS in the 1990s, and when I first showed up in Iowa City to work on that project, she and I had established we remembered each other from the old days and that we knew of the constant manipulation of statistics that always occurred on scoring projects. Heidi and I quickly fell into the easy routine of being annoyed our scorers were so inept but relieved we could conceal their mistakes so easily. The combination of our years of experience in test scoring and the handy new pull button meant there was really no scorer screwup, no matter how horrifying, Heidi and I couldn't make disappear. There was no reliability number, no matter how low, we couldn't fraudulently drag right up into the acceptable range.

By 2007, Pearson's electronic scoring system had been updated enough times that many of the ways I'd known to doctor statistics had been eliminated. No longer could a supervisor improve reliability statistics simply by matching scores in the system that didn't agree, as Greg had first mentioned back in 1994. No longer could the scorers page back to the responses they'd just assessed, which meant it was no longer possible for supervisors to tell their scorers to return to just-completed responses to rescore them another way. No longer could the scorers see when they were second-scoring, which had always allowed them to discuss the papers on their screens with their neighbors, ensuring agreement between them all. Nope, all those tricks had been removed from the system, meaning it might've seemed as if whatever reliability numbers were produced for an item really *would be* the percentage of agreement between the scorers, no longer just a number cooked up by their deadline-driven supervisors.

Those improvements to the system *might* have been construed as proof the industry was trying to do whatever possible to ensure that correct scores were put on student responses and that the resultant agreement statistics were accurate and valid. That *might have been* the case, except for the pull button, which turns out was the simplest way to doctor the stats I'd ever seen. If Heidi and I discovered some response in the system showing a huge disagreement between scorers (like Alice giving a 1 to a response the Boy Genius had already scored a 4), all we had to do was "pull" it out of the system and make it disappear. Heidi would yank the response off the reliability chart, and hence no one would ever know there'd been any alarming disagreement like a 4–1, and then she'd rescore the response before sending it over to my computer to be given a matching score. While it might've been good news we were ultimately getting the correct score put on that response, we were also hiding any evidence of the job our scorers were really doing. Reliability numbers, remember, are only run on a small percentage of responses, and that number is supposed to represent how accurately the scorers are doing on the remaining *thousands* of tests. With the pull button, however, any trace of bad scores and bad reliability statistics could be made to vanish just as completely as did any trace of Saddam Hussein's weapons of mass destruction.

Poof, and they were gone!

As much as I'd come to believe in the folly of large-scale standardized testing, I considered the trip to Iowa in the spring of 2007 an unqualified success. The work had been as foolish as ever, but the return to Iowa City was a homecoming I thoroughly enjoyed. Every day I walked the streets that had once been my home, I visited my favorite bars and bookstores and pizza joints, and I even tried—at more than 40 years old—to recapture past glories at the Hawkeye Soccer Fields.

I had drinks with my good pal Harlan, who still lived in Iowa City and remained a full-time employee of NCS/Pearson/ Pearson Education/Pearson Educational Measurement. Over a bowl of popcorn and a couple of beers at Joe's Place, Harlan and I reminisced about the good ol' days, including the long trips we had taken for NCS's projects. We laughed about some of the things we had seen and done, like the time more than 100 employees had to wait nearly an hour to get into the Tucson scoring center because Harlan, Maria, and I had polished off a bottle of Scotch the night before and subsequently forgotten where we put the building's front-door key.

"Whoops," Harlan smiled, raising his glass to mine.

"And how about some of the scorers?" I asked. "Remember Marvin?"

Of course Harlan remembered Marvin, because Marvin was a longtime scorer in Iowa City who was unforgettable due to his serious alcoholism. Every morning when Marvin got to work, he looked like death, his face pallid and his hands shaking uncontrollably. Most days he wouldn't say a thing in the morning, sitting mutely in front of his computer, clicking away as he scored hundreds of student responses. By the time the first break had passed, however, and by the time Marvin had been out to his car to drink his lunch, finally he started to come around. The color began to come back to Marvin's face, his hands stopped shaking, and he began to be able to string together a lucid sentence or two. For the next couple of hours Marvin was a perfectly good scorer, calm and clearheaded, although by the time of the workday's final break—when he'd been out to his car about four different times— Marvin started to get downright animated. The Marvin who started every day wan and mute ended every day ruddy and rambunctious, a remarkable transformation everyone pretended had no effect at all on the work he was doing.

Harlan shook his head. "Someone should write a book."

I also regularly saw my friend, Maria, who at that point was running a successful testing/consulting business. The two of us got together for nice meals a number of times in Iowa City, sipping martinis and talking about the absurdities we'd witnessed in testing since first working together 13 years before.

"Remember the Guy Who Gave All 2's?" I asked.

Of course Maria remembered the Guy Who Gave All 2's, because he was legendary: The guy had read more than a thousand student responses one day, and not only did he give every single one of them the score of 2—every single one of them!—but when confronted with that fact by the supervisor who discovered it, the Guy Who Gave All 2's didn't even back down. What could he say, he asked? They all seemed like 2's to him. Whether or not one believed that, most amusing about the incident was that the Guy Who Gave All 2's had perfectly acceptable statistics that day. He'd scored a ton of responses, which the company always appreciated, and he'd also given only 2's on a *three*-point scale (1, 2, 3), so deciding every single student response he read earned the default score of 2 meant the Guy Who Gave All 2's had a pretty good reliability percentage that day. Even his disagreements were at least adjacent to whatever score the other scorers had given, and Maria and I shook our heads with wonder about working in an industry where a guy could do a statistically acceptable job without necessarily *reading* any of the student responses he was paid to score.

Maria laughed. "Someone needs to write a book."

"Don't worry," I said to her, as I'd said to Harlan before. "Someone is."

Epilogue

STANDARDIZED testing never did me wrong. For a decade and a half, the industry was nothing but my sugar daddy and travel agent. Working as a consultant for only the first six months of 2005, I made nearly six figures in income, those six figures earned while being my own boss and working either from home or off on some pleasant interstate junket that entailed hotel living and expense account dining. For the easy money alone I should be standardized testing's greatest advocate. And because of the huge increase in work that's resulted from the No Child Left Behind Act, there's no doubt I could earn ever more money each year by continuing to slap down scores onto student responses and penning test passages and questions. I have within my grasp an easy and lucrative career in the industry, and for the rosy future it promises I absolutely should be standardized testing's biggest fan.

I *should be.*

I am not, however, standardized testing's biggest fan. Rather, I am its sworn enemy. It would be disingenuous to suggest otherwise, as I've now spent the better part of two years writing this very book, some 75,000 words I believe illustrate the many, many reasons no one in their right mind would ever entrust decisions about this country's students, teachers, and schools to this industry. I don't know how anyone who's seen what I've seen could come to any other conclusion.

Exactly *what* have I seen that's been so troubling? Let's review.

From my first day in the standardized testing industry (October 1994) until my last day (March 2008), I have watched those assessments be scored with rules that are alternately ambiguous, arbitrary, superficial, and bizarre. That has consistently proven to be the result of trying to establish scoring systems to assess 60,000 (or 100,000, or 10,000) student responses in some standardized way. Maybe one teacher scoring the tests of his or her own 30 students can use a rubric that differentiates rhetorically (a 3 showing "complete understanding," a 2 showing "partial understanding," and a 1 showing "incomplete understanding"), but such a rubric simply never works on a project where the 10 or 20 scorers all have different ideas of what "complete" or "partial" means. Instead, in large-scale assessment we attempt to ensure agreement between the scorers by defining *exactly* what those terms mean, and ultimately, we end up doling out points based less on student comprehension and more on student words. A rubric might tell the scorers to give three points for answers saying "the story is about a statue that tells stories," two points for "the statues tell stories," and one point for "it tells a story"; and we pretend those examples adequately represent the terms *complete*, *partial*, and *incomplete*, pretend they effectively distinguish degrees of comprehension. That is the only thing we can do, because the pressing need to get adequate reliability numbers for every question we score, as well as the race to get projects finished on time, necessitates we use the clearest, if simplest, scoring systems, even if that means we end up with rules that demand crediting one response saying "the Earth rotates" but not a second saying "it rotates."

A scorer once asked if she could credit "she made them" as "she made them by hand," while another wanted to know if he could credit the words "her are closed" as "her eyes are closed."

"Should I," a scorer once asked, "accept 'there is a connection' as 'there is a comparison'?"

"Should I," another questioned, "accept 'what it costs' as 'what it's worth'?"

Day after day, project after project, year after year, those were the questions I fielded as a trainer and those were the distinctions we in the testing industry tried to make. The job wasn't about assessing whether a student had shown "complete" or "incomplete" understanding at all. At its best, the job was only about identifying what random key words in whatever various combinations might have appeared on a student response. Establishing distinct and immutable scoring rules was the only way to do the job with even the hope of getting any agreement within the group, the only chance to assess the responses in any sort of standardized way. For the most part that meant the job entailed making rules and sticking to them—logic be damned!—even if that meant crediting one word ("bubbles") but not a similar word ("sizzles"), while remaining completely unsure about still another one ("fizzes"). That, in sum, was my experience in standardized testing, 15-odd years of debating a dozen or two people about what to do with the response "fizzles" after already having chosen to accept "boils," pretending as we did so that those decisions were really about important ideas like education or student learning, not just something as base as completing a project or meeting a deadline. So, yes, having to score student responses with rules that were dumbed down in the name of expediency and standardization, *that* I did find troubling, absolutely.

What else concerned me? From my first day in the standardized testing industry until my last day, I have watched the open-ended questions on large-scale assessments be scored by temporary employees who could be described as uninterested or unintelligent, apathetic or unemployable. I was a temporary scorer myself, and many of the people who have become my lifelong friends were scorers, too, so I don't mean to be too smug about my own superiority or too unkind about what a bunch of dopes those other people are. Remember, however, whether those scorers are geniuses or dolts, sweethearts or bastards, they *are* doing essential work: they are scoring the tests being used today to decide which students are promoted or graduate, which teachers get raises or bonuses, and which schools or districts get federal education funds. "Professional scorers" have a vitally important job in the current landscape of American education, and it's equally important we frankly address *who* those people are and *why* they do the work they do.

In my case, I got into standardized testing for the extra two bucks an hour, that financial incentive enough to convince me to give up my job filing invoices for another one scoring tests. Most of my friends in Iowa City started careers in testing for the same reason, as scoring work allowed them to maintain lives of happy slacker-dom and grandiose dreams without having to try too hard. It allowed Greg to paint pictures in his girlfriend's basement as he fantasized about a career in the arts, supported Scott as he wrote the screenplay he hoped would someday make him famous, and helped Harlan finance the house on the Mississippi River where he hoped to spend a happy dotage. In Betty's case, she opposed the idea of standardized testing but still agreed to work just to afford her insulin (not even for health insurance, mind you, just cash to buy her meds).

Of course, it is the need for money that motivates most professional scorers, because otherwise no one would ever do such mind-numbing work. Scoring tests is not at all like teaching, a career one might aspire to if he or she were interested in education and perhaps dreamed of helping students learn and grow. Scoring tests is actually more similar to my previous job filing invoices, in which one looks at a piece of paper and classifies it, tossing it into one pile or another, never to think of it again. I didn't ever find the work of scoring tests to be challenging or fulfilling in any way, and the reasons *not* to do it are myriad: The work is short-term (for only weeks or months at a time), pays very little (considerably less than a college degree usually merits), and rarely offers benefits. Plus, the work alternates from being frightfully tedious when scoring the student responses to stressful and demeaning during the training sessions. That monotony was epitomized by the Boy Genius dropping his head in hands and wailing, "It's so booooring" in 2007, and the stress was exemplified in 2005 when a Greek guy named George stomped out of the Phoenix scoring center during one of my training sessions, berating me as he went that I had some gall to doubt his scoring decisions: "I am not wrong!" George screeched. "I have two master's degrees and speak four languages! I cannot always be wrong!"

That, I'm afraid, is the dirty, little secret of the standardized testing industry: The people hired to read and score student responses to standardized tests are, for the most part, people who can't get jobs elsewhere. They are the dregs of the working world, the "uglies and unhirables." Sure, some scorers might agree to the job for the chance to pick up extra cash at a short-term job, but many others are there only because they have no other employment choice. That was always my experience in testing, when the scorers capable of doing a good job moved on to other careers, but the inept settled in for the long haul. On the first project I worked, Vincent was certainly a smart enough fellow to follow any scoring rules, but he did so only while simultaneously studying for the bar exam and only until the day he passed it. Hank, however, who failed to understand or remember many of the scoring rules, had absolutely no other job options available to him, so he stuck around scoring tests inconsistently and incorrectly for another *nine years.*

During my career, I did work with plenty of temporary scorers/supervisors who were both intelligent and accomplished people, including folks working part-time as they went to law school or medical school, teachers working night shifts after a day in the classroom, one guy whose debut short-story collection was already on the shelves of Barnes & Noble, and another running the 400 meters in the Atlanta Olympics. Mostly, however, I worked with people who were not particularly smart or accomplished.

The brilliance of the idea of hiring unemployed people off the streets to work as temporary scorers was best summed up by a guy I worked with in Phoenix. Keith looked like a cartoon strongman, with wide shoulders, a huge barrel chest, and a head shaved clean. He'd just been hired on to score tests for the first time, but Keith said his real job was actually as an "ultimate fighter," those lunatic guys who climb into an octagonal ring and engage in bare-knuckle combat with other similarly minded nut-jobs.

Keith was a nice man, but his mind worked about as quickly as you'd expect from a guy who got punched in the head a lot. He talked slowly and thought slowly, and at lunch every day he would sit at his desk, gazing off into space for half an hour as he ate a can of tuna fish ("for the protein"), apparently not getting bored in the slightest while staring at the wall in front of him for the duration of his break. That lack of a need for mental stimulation, and the inveterate sluggishness with which he talked, thought, or scored, made me think of Keith as an African water buffalo, huge and strong but also slow and dumb. Slow and dumb, unfortunately, was also how I would have characterized Keith's ability to score tests. He turned out to be one of the many temporary employees I wouldn't have wanted trying to figure out what *my* answers on a standardized test might have meant—I'm pretty sure whatever point I was trying to make, Keith wouldn't have got it.

On the final day of the project, however, Keith did end up offering an insight that I found quite trenchant.

"What is it you've been testing me for, anyway?" he asked.

"Excuse me?" I replied.

"These tests you're giving me, are they psychological?" Keith said. "Are you trying to figure out if I'm sane?"

I looked at Keith and saw he wasn't kidding. While for three weeks Keith had been sitting in front of a computer scoring student responses, he seemed to believe that somehow *he* was being tested, not that the students were.

"You're not being tested, Keith," I told him. "You are grading the students who have already taken this science test."

He looked at me blankly.

"The answers you've been reading," I continued, "are how the students responded to those questions, and the scores you've been clicking into the computer are your assessment on how well they did."

Keith continued to look at me blankly, so I tried once more. "You are deciding whether or not the students have done a good job."

"*I'm* deciding if kids are smart or not?" he asked.

"Yes, you are."

"*Me?*" Keith said, shaking his head in disbelief. "Wow."

Wow indeed. Day after day, project after project, year after year, those were the people I worked with scoring tests, temporary employees of varying degrees of intelligence and accomplishment but overwhelmingly a population like Keith and Michi and Alice and Hank, people I wouldn't have been too happy deciding my fate. At the end of the 2008–2009 school year, the standardized testing industry will process nearly 60 million tests, so how surprising can it be that many of those tests will end up being read and scored by such people? Really, how many smart and conscientious college-educated people do we imagine there are on America's unemployment lines, how many folks willing to suck it up to be bored and demeaned working for a paltry hourly wage? I'd say not a lot, as mostly what I saw in standardized testing was a codependent relationship between the companies that have millions of tests to be scored (willing to hire almost anyone they can to get the job done) and the unemployed folks who have college degrees but not enough sense to really make use of them (willing to take whatever job is available). So, yes, entrusting decisions about this country's students, teachers, and schools to an industry populated with temporary employees largely incapable of getting real jobs, *that* did concern me, absolutely.

What else bothered me? From my first day in standardized testing until my last day, I have worked in a business seemingly more concerned with getting scores put on student responses than getting *meaningful* scores put on them, a reality that can't be too surprising given the massive scope of the assessment industry and the limited time available to score those tests. Consider if there are 20 short-answer/essay questions on each of the 60 million tests mentioned earlier. That means there would be 1.2 *billion* student responses that would need to be read and scored during the 2007–2008 school year. Remember also that most testing occurs in the springtime, meaning many of those 1.2 *billion* student responses would need to be read and scored within the same two- or three-month time frame. Given those staggering numbers, how surprising can it be that in 2001 the *New York Times* quoted education consultant Nina Metzner as saying her experience in large-scale assessment revealed an industry spread too thin, her work scoring tests characterized by "a lack of personnel, a lack of time, too many projects, and too few people." While Metzner's quote might be worrisome on its own, even more disturbing is the fact she said it eight years ago, even before the mandate of the No Child Left Behind Act so massively increased the demands on today's testing industry.

My time in testing confirms Metzner's quote, as most of my career seemed like a desperate push to get things done, more greasing the wheels of commerce than any earnest educational endeavor. On the very first project I worked, my starting date was pushed back one day, two days, three days, four, until we finally started working a week after originally scheduled. That meant our six weeks of scoring work actually became only five, and while that managed to cost us scorers money, it also meant we had to rush to finish on time. It meant near the final days of the "sixth" week we were told to score faster, ask fewer questions, work longer hours, to just keep putting those damned scores on the student responses. A job that might have begun thoughtfully and conscientiously eventually devolved into a race to make the deadline, and to think the tests scored in the last weeks of the project were given the same consideration as those scored in the first weeks is no more than a fantasy.

That need to get things done was the primary motivation for most of the malfeasances I witnessed or was party to during my career in standardized testing. It was the reason Roseanne, to the detriment of the students she was supposed to care for, blithely changed the scoring of the student essays halfway through her state's "focused holistic" writing project, as her only other option would have been to throw out the first two weeks of scoring and began the whole process anew, an idea so costly and time-consuming it was inconceivable. It was the reason the NAEP writing range-finding committee changed the way it had been scoring to match the predictions of the ETS psychometricians, even though the committee consisted mainly of educators brought in expressly for their writing expertise, while the psychometricians had actually never even seen the student responses. It was the reason the industry established foolish rules on scoring projects ("Trend Tests must be administered after every 30-minute break") and then proceeded to ignore them ("Enjoy your 29-minute, 55-second lunch!").

That need to get things done was the reason my firing from that first writing project (for failing the qualifying tests) lasted but 12 hours, only until the company realized they were short on personnel. It was the reason I cheated or helped others cheat on the qualifying tests of every subsequent scoring project I ever worked on, because we *always* had concerns about having enough personnel. It was the reason I was told on more than one occasion to be sure my teams didn't do "too good a job" scoring the student responses, because then teams in future years might have too hard a time duplicating our high reliability. It was the reason I saw a temporary employee get reprimanded one year for too obviously manipulating the reliability statistics and then subsequently get hired as a full-time project manager.

Day after day, project after project, year after year, my job was focused on completing tasks and meeting deadlines, but nothing any more exalted than that. That was obvious at the most recent scoring project I worked on, in March 2008 in Virginia Beach, where I saw a poster hanging on the scoring center wall that summed up what standardized test scoring was truly all about. "Productivity!" the poster blared, defining that concept with a picture of a cartoon guy using a cartoon bow to fire cartoon arrows at a cartoon target painted with the numbers 6, 5, 4, 3, 2, and 1. Above the archer was the word *reliability*, and above the target was the word *validity*, while above those two words hung the phrase "Gettin' stuff done." At that scoring center, apparently "productivity" meant "gettin' stuff done." While I thought the comic-strip poster was pretty foolish, I appreciated that at least it was honest about the work that was really occurring. The "productivity" poster showed quite clearly that the scoring of standardized tests wasn't an exact science at all, just some freaky guy (Hank? Keith? Me?) choosing numbers based less on any scientific system than just the variables and vagaries of lobbing missiles in the air—wherever the arrow came down, the poster was saying, there was your student's score. So, yes, working in an industry where "validity" and "reliability" weren't lofty ideals at all but just a couple of words that fell under the umbrella of "gettin' stuff done," *that* did bother me, absolutely.

Anything else about standardized testing that disturbed me? Well, mostly my sincere belief it doesn't work. Certainly the assessment industry works in terms of writing, editing, printing, shipping, scoring, returning, and reporting millions and millions of tests every year, and it works in terms of drumming up approximately a billion dollars of business a year for some of the country's big, fat corporations, but I'm not convinced all that paper pushing and money making amounts to much in terms of education. I understand the testing industry does produce a lot of data, and I understand that data result from the answers students give to assessments being administered all over this country, but that still doesn't mean I believe those resultant statistics accurately reflect the specific abilities of America's students, teachers, or schools. Uh-uh. No way.

I don't believe the results because the industry is too big for its own good, basically too many cooks in the kitchen spoiling the broth. One year I worked for ETS building anchor sets that would later be used to train the professional scorers, but the next year the government agency in charge decided those training sets would be built by Pearson *under the supervision* of ETS. That meant the Pearson employees would build the training sets but needed ETS's approval on them, so in effect I sat around all day as some Pearson person tried to put together the training sets I wanted built. I spent my days twiddling my thumbs half the time while spending my remaining hours trying to convince some Pearson person how I wanted the job done, trying to explain a pretty inexplicable process instead of just doing it myself. If that Pearson employee failed to build the sets the way I wanted, I sent that person back to a cubicle to try again while I spent most of the day trolling the Internet. It was an absurd scenario, labor-intensive and time-consuming, and at some point I joked what the situation really needed was the involvement of a *third* company, a comment that ended up being less comical than clairvoyant when that third organization did arrive on the scene, an oversight company sent by the government to act as a liaison between ETS and Pearson.

Having all those people and all those companies involved in the test-scoring process still didn't change the ugly truth about the work. One day when I stood in front of my nine temporary employees in Iowa City in 2007, I was also watched by seven industry big-wigs, those VIPs there to persuade themselves about the merit of the work. The seven guests included one member of the ETS management team, two members of the Pearson management team, one representative of the U.S. government agency responsible for the test's development, another from a second U.S. government agency in charge of testing oversight, and two independent consultants hired to oversee quality assurance. It was a mighty impressive display of the educational elite in the cubicle that morning, an awesome array of credentials that would have cowed anyone who dared doubt the mighty power of the standardized test, but in the end that masquerade didn't last too long. After only a couple of hours of watching, the experts had seen enough to be convinced of the legitimacy of our work and hence left the scoring center forever, thereby entrusting the fates of America's students, teachers, and schools to the sage judgments of my scorers Alice, Michi, Abdullah, Bill, et al.

I don't believe the results of standardized testing because most of the major players in the industry are for-profit enterprises that—even if they do have the word *education* in their names—are pretty clearly in the business as much to make big bucks as to make good tests. Although the perception might be that all those companies are collaborators who care only for the greater educational good, in truth they are competitors angling for the same contracts and the same dollars, a dynamic made clear early in my career when one boss at NCS told me we wouldn't be dining that evening with our ETS peers because, she said, "We don't cavort with the enemy." I once read an intercompany memo discussing an upcoming scoring project that concluded with the bullet "Relations between Pearson, ETS, and NCES will remain cordial and collegial"— and what is an instruction stipulating how people should behave except a tacit admission that once they did not? One time I sat in a meeting between representatives of a state department of education and the testing company contracted to write its tests, and the fact the testing company's primary motivation was economic was never in doubt. When the representatives of the state DOE complained about the quality of the items being put on their tests and demanded new ones be written, the testing company spokesman waved a paper in the air while shaking his head no.

"Sorry," he said, not seeming sorry at all. "I have a contract here signed by your state superintendent that confirms we can use the questions already existing in our item bank to build your test, and that's what we're going to do." Although the testing rep smiled at the members of the state DOE, it wasn't necessarily a friendly gesture, more an announcement that the testing company—with its signed contract already in hand—was going to get away with whatever it could, the quality of the test or the desires of those DOE representatives be damned. Because the testing company was a for-profit business, I wasn't surprised they wanted to recycle the questions already in their item bank instead of paying someone to write new ones, as I was never surprised during my time in testing when any company opted for expediency or profit over the quality of the work.

I don't believe the results of standardized testing because "intelligence" and "teaching experience" turned out not to be attributes one would want in a professional scorer but rather faults in them that needed to be overcome. The job of test scoring really only involves learning and following the simplistic rules someone else has established. I always hoped my teams would consist of people who were smart enough to understand the rules but not so smart they'd be inclined to disagree with them. Once in Iowa City I had a brilliant scorer who was only working part-time as he went to medical school, but Carlos's daunting intelligence was a serious inconvenience in my attempts to train my group. He was always making the sort of insightful and informed arguments about student responses that really had no place at the scoring center. For the most part Carlos's arguments were so damned complex they simply confused his teammates or made them want to cry.

"I don't see how we can give full credit to Anchor Paper #3 without also giving full credit to Anchor Paper #5," he said one day. "In terms of Boolean logic—"

"Ha!" I laughed aloud, interrupting him. I didn't mean to laugh, but I couldn't help it. While Carlos may have been making a perfectly good point, I found his rationalization for that point absolutely hilarious. Carlos wanted to discuss the scores given to two 10th graders in terms of "Boolean logic," while beside him sat a scorer who had tried to read from a rubric she held upside down. I didn't even know what "Boolean logic" was, and the idea my team of dear, dumb scorers might have known was absolutely priceless, so eventually I had to tell Carlos *he* could score however he wanted, but I needed the rest of the team to follow the original and simple scoring rules already established. It was all they could manage, I told Carlos, so he'd have to keep his perfectly good arguments to himself, if only to save a number of his teammates from having their heads explode. Boolean logic! It makes me laugh to this day.

Teachers or ex-teachers who became professional scorers were equally problematic, for a couple of reasons. Many of them used to make huge leaps when reading the student responses, convinced they knew what a student was saying even if that didn't match the words on the page.

"I get it," some former teacher would tell me. "When this kid says 'not right' on his bike safety poster, he really means 'it's not right to ride on the right side.'"

"Does it say that anywhere?" I would ask.

"Of course not," the teacher would say, smiling as if I were quite slow. "But that's what it means."

"Sorry," I'd say. "You aren't supposed to *find* the points. You can only credit what is obviously there, what 8 of 10 people would see."

The tendency of those current or former educators to look so hard for credit in the student responses, plus their tendency to give thoughtful readings to them, was frankly the bane of my existence. If I was standing in front of a group of 10 or 20 scorers, the last thing I needed was for each to be giving a meticulous and earnest review to every student response. Meticulous and earnest reviews of every student response meant the scorers might never agree with each other (one scorer might find some esoteric nugget of wisdom in a single word of the first sentence, while perhaps another would find some major fault in the second), and the scorers agreeing with each other was the *primary* purpose of standardized test scoring. I didn't need scorers spending five minutes looking for the hidden truth in every response; I needed them to look for key words and slap down a quick score. People who were too smart or cared too much were certainly not the people who helped most in that regard, and hence I found myself hoping for a team of scorers that was neither too brainy nor too invested in the state of American education.

I don't believe the results of standardized testing because it is the most inexact of sciences. At some point when scoring an item saying the football player Dallas was "shy" might not be worth any points, but later—after further consideration of the third paragraph of the second page of the story—that word might not seem so unreasonable and could be awarded credit after all. That would mean some student responses would earn points for the word *shy* but earlier responses would *not* have been given the same credit, an inconsistency that was no more than an unfortunate reality of the standardized testing business. The thought process changed, so the scores changed—*c'est la vie.*

Scores changed because opinions changed, and at least for open-ended questions, the scoring of standardized tests is largely a matter of opinion. That's not so much the case in multiple-choice testing, because those questions are more factual:

1. The first shots of the U.S. Civil War were fired at what location?
   A. Pearl Harbor
   B. Fort Sumter
   C. Lexington and Concord
   D. Appomattox Court House

Because it is a historical fact that the first shots of the U.S. Civil War were fired at Fort Sumter, there's no doubt that B is the correct answer to this question. Such clarity, however, usually doesn't exist when assessing open-ended items:

The U.S. Civil War was fought in the years 1861 to 1865 between the United States and the Confederate States of America. Explain one of the causes of that war.

In academic circles to this day there remains debate about the causes of the Civil War, and hence when some group of teachers or test experts convened to write a rubric for an open-ended question like this one, they often didn't come to a final, firm, and indisputable conclusion about a question's "correct" answer. Some of the rubric writers might argue slavery was the cause, while others might have offered states' rights, economic inequality, or the simple need to preserve the Union as their choice. Regardless, disagreement among the experts often ensued about how to mete out points to the student responses. Given those experts couldn't always agree how to score the open-ended questions, how surprising can it be that it was necessary to doctor the reliability statistics to make it appear as if our not-so-well-informed scorers could?

Such uncertainty was nearly always evident when committees of teachers came together, whether it was a development meeting when those educators were writing test questions or a range-finding meeting where they were trying to establish or approve scoring systems. Differing opinions were always prevalent. In my time in testing, I consistently worked with committees that disagreed with former committees, committees that disagreed with each other within a committee, and committees that often ended up even disagreeing with themselves. Differing opinions were why those teachers on my first range-finding committee demanded to know "who wrote these questions," that group of classroom teachers utterly aghast at what a previous group of classroom teachers had once done. Differing opinions were why it sometimes took as much as 30 minutes to score a single student essay during the first NAEP writing range-finding committee I worked on, because words on the rubric like *skillful* or *sufficient* were much more subjective than they were concrete. Differing opinions were the reason we at the testing companies would roll our eyes every time some group of teachers ended up complaining yet again about the quality of the questions *they* had written three months before. Meanwhile, amid all the differing opinions, and amid all the score changes and rules changes, the assessment industry was ostensibly doing the work of "standardized" testing.

It is that name that upsets me most about the "standardized" testing industry, because I never found anything even remotely standardized about the work. In fact, if you were to ask me to describe it, I would say standardized testing is akin to a scientific experiment in which everything is a variable. Everything. It seems to me the score given to every response, and ultimately the final results given to each student, depended as much on the vagaries of the testing industry as they did on the quality of the student answers. From my experience, those scores and those results would depend on who wrote the questions and who established the scoring rules. From my experience, those student scores and student results would depend on the scoring center where a test was assessed, whether one in Iowa City populated mostly with liberal whites, one in Arizona filled with conservative senior citizens, or one in Virginia peopled more with African Americans and military personnel. From my experience, those student scores and student results would depend on what point in a project a test was assessed (either before some rule got changed or after), what time of the day it was read (hopefully not until after the morning coffee had kicked in, but before the fog of daily boredom had crashed down), and what cubicle it was sent to (one with a trainer who was more stringent in interpreting the scoring rules, or perhaps another with a trainer who had a more tolerant perspective). Ultimately, of course, those student scores and student results would depend on which professional scorer assessed each student response, whether one of the rare ones like Carlos or the Boy Genius who actually understood the rules and doled out the points accordingly or, more likely, one of the legions of drunks, dingbats, and dilettantes I worked with over the years who pretty much had no idea how they were supposed to be scoring.

In my opinion, the industry isn't "standardized" in any way, and I don't believe the results. Reading a 2006 story in the *Boston Globe* excitedly touting the improvements of inner-city kids in Massachusetts, I simply thought, "I don't believe." Reading a 2006 story in the *New York Post* about one local school district moving toward a year-round school calendar because it did poorly on state tests in relation to neighboring schools, I simply thought, "I don't believe." Reading a 2007 story in the *New York Times* about how the New York City Department of Education had started out giving bonuses to teachers based largely on the results of state tests, I simply thought, "I don't believe." My default position about any test results getting returned to students, teachers, or schools is "I don't believe."

What I do believe is that if a student gets a score back for any assessment that includes open-ended questions, that result is only one of the many theoretical possibilities that exists for that test—I don't believe it is *the* score of a test, simply *a* score. I believe if a student was told he or she earned a 37 out of a possible 50 points on a test, after rescoring that very test might well be scored a 41, or a 33, or a 38, or a 34, or a 42, or a 35, ad infinitum. I don't necessarily believe the overall score for that test would change radically all the way from a 37 to a 12, for instance, but I do believe the final score given to any standardized test including open-ended questions would fluctuate significantly based on any of the many factors mentioned here. Fifteen years of scoring standardized tests has completely convinced me as much: that the business I've worked in is less a precise tool to assess students' exact abilities than just a lucrative means to make indefinite and indistinct generalizations about them. The idea standardized testing can make any sort of fine distinction about students—a very particular and specific commentary on their individual skills and abilities that a classroom teacher was unable to make—seems like folderol to me, absolute folderol.

What does it really mean to entrust decisions about this country's students, teachers, and schools to the massive standardized testing industry? In my opinion, it means trusting an industry that is unashamedly in the business of making money instead of listening to the many people who went into education for the more altruistic desire to do good. It means giving credence to the thoughts of mobs of temporary employees who only dabble in assessment while ignoring the opinions of the men and women who dedicate themselves daily to the world of teaching and learning. It means saying you're not interested in what the Mrs. White or Mr. Reyes who stands in front of a classroom of children every day might think about their students' progress, but you're absolutely enthralled to hear the thoughts on that same subject of a dopey Hank, a non-English-speaking Michi, a senile Alice, or a uninterested Todd. It means ignoring the conclusions about student abilities of this country's teachers—the people who instruct and nurture this country's children every single day—to instead heed the snap judgments of bored temps giving fleeting glances to student work.

I understand people may disagree with me, but none of that sounds like too good an idea to me. It seems to me entrusting the education of this country's children to "professional scorers" in far distant states instead of the men and women who stand in front of their classrooms each day is about as smart an idea as entrusting your health not to the doctor holding a stethoscope to your heart but to some accountant crunching numbers in Omaha. Personally, I'd trust the guy who's looking me in the eye.

If *I* had to take any standardized test today that was important to my future and would be assessed by the scoring processes I have long been a part of, I promise you I would protest; I would fight; I would sue; I would go on a hunger strike or march on Washington. I might even punch someone in the nose, but I would never allow that massive and ridiculous business to have any say in my future without battling it to the bitter, bitter end.

Do what you want, America, but at least you have been warned.

Index

About the Author

AFTER AN "interesting" career in standardized testing, Todd Farley became a freelance writer, earning bylines in publications as varied as *Education Week*, *Rethinking Schools*, *Neurology Now*, *Working Waterfront*, *Port City Life*, *New York Press*, and *Hustler*. *Making the Grades: My Misadventures in the Standardized Testing Industry* is Farley's first book, but he hopes there will be others. Todd lives with his family in New York City.

Other Books from PoliPointPress

The Blue Pages: A Directory of Companies Rated by Their Politics and Practices
Helps consumers match their buying decisions with their political values by listing the political contributions and business practices of over 1,000 companies. $9.95, paperback.

Sasha Abramsky, *Breadline USA: The Hidden Scandal of American Hunger and How to Fix It*
Treats the increasing food insecurity crisis in America not only as a matter of failed policies, but also as an issue of real human suffering. $23.95, cloth.

Rose Aguilar, *Red Highways: A Liberal's Journey into the Heartland*
Challenges red state stereotypes to reveal new strategies for progressives. $15.95, paperback.

Dean Baker, *Plunder and Blunder: The Rise and Fall of the Bubble Economy*
Chronicles the growth and collapse of the stock and housing bubbles and explains how policy blunders and greed led to the catastrophic—but completely predictable—market meltdowns. $15.95, paperback.

Jeff Cohen, *Cable News Confidential: My Misadventures in Corporate Media*
Offers a fast-paced romp through the three major cable news channels—Fox CNN, and MSNBC—and delivers a serious message about their failure to cover the most urgent issues of the day. $14.95, paperback.

Marjorie Cohn, *Cowboy Republic: Six Ways the Bush Gang Has Defied the Law*
Shows how the executive branch under President Bush has systematically defied the law instead of enforcing it. $14.95, paperback.

Marjorie Cohn and Kathleen Gilberd, *Rules of Disengagement: The Politics and Honor of Military Dissent*
Examines what U.S. military men and women have done—and what their families and others can do—to resist illegal wars, as well

as military racism, sexual harassment, and denial of proper medical care. $14.95, paperback.

Joe Conason, *The Raw Deal: How the Bush Republicans Plan to Destroy Social Security and the Legacy of the New Deal*
Reveals the well-financed and determined effort to undo the Social Security Act and other New Deal programs. $11.00, paperback.

Kevin Danaher, Shannon Biggs, and Jason Mark, *Building the Green Economy: Success Stories from the Grassroots*
Shows how community groups, families, and individual citizens have protected their food and water, cleaned up their neighborhoods, and strengthened their local economies. $16.00, paperback.

Kevin Danaher and Alisa Gravitz, *The Green Festival Reader: Fresh Ideas from Agents of Change*
Collects the best ideas and commentary from some of the most forward green thinkers of our time. $15.95, paperback.

Reese Erlich, *Dateline Havana: The Real Story of U.S. Policy and the Future of Cuba*
Explores Cuba's strained relationship with the United States, the island nation's evolving culture and politics, and prospects for U.S. Cuba policy with the departure of Fidel Castro. $22.95, hardcover.

Reese Erlich, *The Iran Agenda: The Real Story of U.S. Policy and the Middle East Crisis*
Explores the turbulent recent history between the two countries and how it has led to a showdown over nuclear technology. $14.95, paperback.

Todd Farley, *Making the Grades: My Misadventures in the Standardized Testing Industry*
Exposes the folly of many large-scale educational assessments through an alternately edifying and hilarious first-hand account of life in the testing business. $16.95, paperback.

Steven Hill, *10 Steps to Repair American Democracy*
Identifies the key problems with American democracy, especially election practices, and proposes ten specific reforms to reinvigorate it. $11.00, paperback.

Jim Hunt, *They Said What? Astonishing Quotes on American Power, Democracy, and Dissent*
Covering everything from squashing domestic dissent to stymieing equal representation, these quotes remind progressives exactly what they're up against. $12.95, paperback.

Michael Huttner and Jason Salzman, *50 Ways You Can Help Obama Change America*
Describes actions citizens can take to clean up the mess from the last administration, enact Obama's core campaign promises, and move the country forward. $12.95, paperback.

Markos Kounalakis and Peter Laufer, *Hope Is a Tattered Flag: Voices of Reason and Change for the Post-Bush Era*
Gathers together the most listened-to politicos and pundits, activists and thinkers, to answer the question: what happens after Bush leaves office? $29.95, hardcover; $16.95 paperback.

Yvonne Latty, *In Conflict: Iraq War Veterans Speak Out on Duty, Loss, and the Fight to Stay Alive*
Features the unheard voices, extraordinary experiences, and personal photographs of a broad mix of Iraq War veterans, including Congressman Patrick Murphy, Tammy Duckworth, Kelly Daugherty, and Camilo Mejia. $24.00, hardcover.

Phillip Longman, *Best Care Anywhere: Why VA Health Care Is Better Than Yours*
Shows how the turnaround at the long-maligned VA hospitals provides a blueprint for salvaging America's expensive but troubled health care system. $14.95, paperback.

Phillip Longman and Ray Boshara, *The Next Progressive Era*
Provides a blueprint for a re-empowered progressive movement and describes its implications for families, work, health, food, and savings. $22.95, hardcover.

Marcia and Thomas Mitchell, *The Spy Who Tried to Stop a War: Katharine Gun and the Secret Plot to Sanction the Iraq Invasion*
Describes a covert operation to secure UN authorization for the Iraq war and the furor that erupted when a young British spy leaked it. $23.95, hardcover.

Susan Mulcahy, ed., *Why I'm a Democrat*
Explores the values and passions that make a diverse group of Americans proud to be Democrats. $14.95, paperback.

David Neiwert, *The Eliminationists: How Hate Talk Radicalized the American Right*
Argues that the conservative movement's alliances with far-right extremists have not only pushed the movement's agenda to the right, but also have become a malignant influence increasingly reflected in political discourse. $16.95, paperback.

Christine Pelosi, *Campaign Boot Camp: Basic Training for Future Leaders*
Offers a seven-step guide for successful campaigns and causes at all levels of government. $15.95, paperback.

William Rivers Pitt, *House of Ill Repute: Reflections on War, Lies, and America's Ravaged Reputation*
Skewers the Bush Administration for its reckless invasions, warrantless wiretaps, lethally incompetent response to Hurricane Katrina, and other scandals and blunders. $16.00, paperback.

Sarah Posner, *God's Profits: Faith, Fraud, and the Republican Crusade for Values Voters*
Examines corrupt televangelists' ties to the Republican Party and unprecedented access to the Bush White House. $19.95, hardcover.

Nomi Prins, *Jacked: How "Conservatives" Are Picking Your Pocket –Whether You Voted for Them or Not*
Describes how the "conservative" agenda has affected your wallet, skewed national priorities, and diminished America—but not the American spirit. $12.00, paperback.

Cliff Schecter, *The Real McCain: Why Conservatives Don't Trust Him—And Why Independents Shouldn't*
Explores the gap between the public persona of John McCain and the reality of this would-be president.
$14.95, hardcover.

Norman Solomon, *Made Love, Got War: Close Encounters with America's Warfare State*
Traces five decades of American militarism and the media's all-too-frequent failure to challenge it. $24.95, hardcover.

John Sperling et al., *The Great Divide: Retro vs. Metro America*
Explains how and why our nation is so bitterly divided into what the authors call Retro and Metro America. $19.95, paperback.

Daniel Weintraub, *Party of One: Arnold Schwarzenegger and the Rise of the Independent Voter*
Explains how Schwarzenegger found favor with independent voters, whose support has been critical to his success, and suggests that his bipartisan approach represents the future of American politics. $19.95, hardcover.

Curtis White, *The Barbaric Heart: Faith, Money, and the Crisis of Nature*
Argues that the solution to the present environmental crisis may come from an unexpected quarter: the arts, religion, and the realm of the moral imagination.
$16.95, paperback.

Curtis White, *The Spirit of Disobedience: Resisting the Charms of Fake Politics, Mindless Consumption, and the Culture of Total Work*
Debunks the notion that liberalism has no need for spirituality and describes a "middle way" through our red state/blue state political impasse. Includes three powerful interviews with John DeGraaf, James Howard Kunstler, and Michael Ableman. $24.00, hardcover.

For more information, please visit www.p3books.com.

About This Book

This book is printed on Cascade Enviro100 Print paper. It contains 100 percent post-consumer fiber and is certified EcoLogo, Processed Chlorine Free, and FSC Recycled. For each ton used instead of virgin paper, we:

Save the equivalent of 17 trees
Reduce air emissions by 2,098 pounds
Reduce solid waste by 1,081 pounds
Reduce the water used by 10,196 gallons
Reduce suspended particles in the water by 6.9 pounds.

This paper is manufactured using biogas energy, reducing natural gas consumption by 2,748 cubic feet per ton of paper produced.

The book's printer, Malloy Incorporated, works with paper mills that are environmentally responsible, that do not source fiber from endangered forests, and that are third-party certified. Malloy prints with soy and vegetable based inks, and over 98 percent of the solid material they discard is recycled. Their water emissions are entirely safe for disposal into their municipal sanitary sewer system, and they work with the Michigan Department of Environmental Quality to ensure that their air emissions meet all environmental standards.

The Michigan Department of Environmental Quality has recognized Malloy as a Great Printer for their compliance with environmental regulations, written environmental policy, pollution prevention efforts, and pledge to share best practices with other printers. Their county Department of Planning and Environment has designated them a Waste Knot Partner for their waste prevention and recycling programs.